BTEC Level 3 National Study Skills Guide in Business

Welcome to your Study Skills Guide! You can make it your own – start by adding your personal and course details below...

Learner's name: _____

BTEC course title: _____

Date started: _____

Mandatory units:

_____

_____

_____

Optional units:

_____

_____

_____

Centre name: _____

Centre address:

_____

_____

_____

Tutor's name: _____

Published by Pearson Education Limited, a company incorporated in England and Wales, having its registered office at Edinburgh Gate, Harlow, Essex, CM20 2JE. Registered company number: 872828

Edexcel is a registered trademark of Edexcel Limited

Text © Pearson Education Limited 2010

First published 2010

17 16 15

17 16 15

British Library Cataloguing in Publication Data

A catalogue record for this book is available from the British Library

ISBN 978 1 84690 562 9

Typeset and edited by Ken Vail Graphic Design, Cambridge
Cover design by Visual Philosophy, created by eMC Design
Cover photo/illustration © Alamy/Image Source Black
Printed and bound by L.E.G.O. S.p.A. Lavis (TN) - Italy

Acknowledgements

The author and publisher would like to thank the following individuals and organisations for permission to reproduce photographs:

Alamy Images: Angela Hampton Picture Library 19, Claudia Wiens 62;
Corbis: 72; **iStockphoto:** Jaimie Duplass 15, Chris Schmidt 33, Jeffrey Smith 10; **Pearson Education Ltd:** Ian Wedgewood 55; **Pearson Education Ltd:** Steve Shott 28; **Shutterstock:** Lisa F. Young 80

Cover images: *Front:* **Corbis:** Bill Varie

All other images © Pearson Education

Every effort has been made to contact copyright holders of material reproduced in this book. Any omissions will be rectified in subsequent printings if notice is given to the publishers.

Websites

Go to www.pearsonhotlinks.co.uk to gain access to the relevant website links and information on how they can aid your studies. When you access the site, search for either the title BTEC Level 3 National Study Skills Guide in Business or ISBN 9781846905629.

Disclaimer

This material has been published on behalf of Edexcel and offers high-quality support for the delivery of Edexcel qualifications.

This does not mean that the material is essential to achieve any Edexcel qualification, nor does it mean that it is the only suitable material available to support any Edexcel qualification. Edexcel material will not be used verbatim in setting any Edexcel examination or assessment. Any resource lists produced by Edexcel shall include this and other appropriate resources.

Copies of official specifications for all Edexcel qualifications may be found on the Edexcel website: www.edexcel.com

Contents

Popular progression pathways

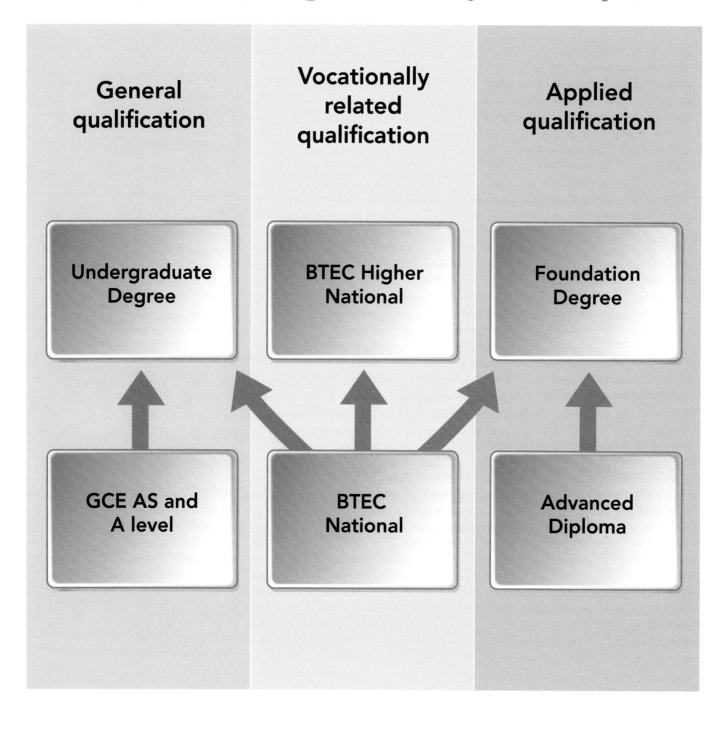

Ten steps to success in your BTEC Level 3 National

This Study Skills Guide has been written to help you achieve the best result possible on your BTEC Level 3 National course. At the start of a new course you may feel both quite excited but also a little apprehensive. Taking a BTEC Level 3 National qualification has many benefits and is a major stepping stone towards your future career. Using this Study Skills Guide will help you get the most out of your course from the start.

TOP TIP

Use this Study Skills Guide at your own pace. Dip in to find what you need. Look back at it whenever you have a problem or query.

During **induction** sessions at the start of your course, your tutor will explain important information, but it can be difficult to remember everything and that's when you'll find this Study Skills Guide invaluable. Look at it whenever you want to check anything related to your course. It provides all the essential facts you need and has a Useful terms section to explain specialist terms, words and phrases, including some that you will see highlighted in this book in bold type.

This Study Skills Guide covers the skills you'll need to do well in your course – such as managing your time, researching and analysing information and preparing a presentation.

- Use the **Top tips** to make your life easier as you go.
- Use the **Key points** to help you to stay focused on the essentials.
- Use the **Action points** to check what you need to know or do now.
- Use the **Case studies** to relate information to your chosen sector and vocational area.

- Use the **Activities** to test your knowledge and skills.
- Use the **Useful terms** section to check the meaning of specialist terms.

This Study Skills Guide has been designed to work alongside the Edexcel Student Book for BTEC Level 3 National Business (Edexcel, 2010). This Student Book includes the main knowledge you'll need, with tips from BTEC experts, Edexcel assignment tips, assessment activities and up-to-date case studies from industry experts, plus handy references to your Study Skills Guide.

This Study Skills Guide is divided into ten steps, each relating to a key aspect of your studies, from understanding assessment to time management to maximising opportunities. Concentrate on getting things right one step at a time. Thousands of learners have achieved BTEC Level 3 National qualifications and are now studying for a degree, or building a successful career at work. Using this Study Skills Guide, and believing in your own abilities, will help you achieve your future goals, too.

Introduction to the business sector

The business sector covers a large range of occupations and professions and, through your BTEC Level 3 National in Business, you will become aware of the variety of interesting opportunities that BTEC qualifications can lead to.

The course will give you the opportunity, not only to learn about the world of business, but also to apply your knowledge to real-life business situations. Completing the course may enable you to go on to higher education, or you may choose to pursue employment straightaway.

Once you enter the world of work you will quickly understand how important the business sector is to the UK economy. Business in the profit-making part of the sector is about the creation of wealth; if businesses cannot achieve this goal, the UK economy overall will suffer.

The UK business sector

The contribution that businesses make to the UK economy is significant. Currently, over 75% of the contribution made to the UK economy by businesses comes from the Service Sector – any business that provides a service, such as hotels, retailers and financial institutions. Manufacturing businesses make up about 13% of the business contribution and the remainder comes from other industries, such as agriculture. Your BTEC National in Business will allow you to examine this situation and consider questions about important issues, such as our economic future.

The business sector relies heavily on innovation, enterprise and the development of small businesses. Napoleon supposedly remarked that the British are 'a nation of shopkeepers' and he was right, in as much as Britain is a nation of small and medium-sized enterprises (SMEs). You could say that these SMEs are the backbone of Britain – the UK economy consists of 99% SMEs. Of the 4.8 million businesses operating in the UK, fewer than 1% are large corporations, that is with over 250 employees.

Many believe that the British Government has a tendency to overlook the SME Sector, as it tends to be quite fragmented. Yet, it is precisely this sector that provides the vital and fertile seedbed, from where tomorrow's large corporations will emerge. If the UK is able to improve its SME performance, this will have a substantially positive effect on the entire UK economy.

The pace of change in the business world continues to increase; what was satisfactory yesterday is no longer wanted today or may be superseded by something better tomorrow. Globalisation, competition from developing countries, the speed of communication, the advance of technology and rapidly altering consumer tastes are driving this change.

The role of business is to create wealth (or add value). This added value is used to reward stakeholders – employees, providers of capital, and Government through corporation tax – and then to sustain and develop the business through investment for growth. The UK business sector has to invest in new and better products and services, requiring businesses and people to be innovative. New and better products may be created by new technology or design, a new application of old technology, through a new delivery model or just by improving business processes. The ability to create new ideas, evaluate them, and use knowledge and skill to develop them is fundamental to a business's innovative success.

As you start work in this sector, you will be entering an environment which is truly dynamic and has endless opportunities. A BTEC National in Business will teach you about the different aspects of running a business, allowing you to make informed choices about your future.

What you will learn about

There are now four 'sizes' of BTEC National in Business! The Subsidiary Diploma has two mandatory units, and the Certificate, Diploma and Extended Diploma all have four mandatory units. In these units you will:

- learn about the business environment by examining the various types of business, looking at how the external environment helps to shape their activities
- look at how a business obtains resources – physical, financial and human – and how they are managed effectively
- learn about customers and the drive to meet customer needs through marketing methods
- examine how effective communication is vital for organisational success, both within the business and from the business to the outside world.

There are numerous optional units which your centre may offer including:

- Finance – the 'blood' of the business which allows all activities to take place; you will examine how finance is raised and managed to keep the business moving forward

- Marketing – which examines how building long-term relationships with customers can provide significant benefits
- People issues – how a business's staff is the most important resource; staff must be recruited carefully, and then trained and developed to perform well
- Legal aspects of running a business
- Impact of communications technology
- The world of retailing.

How you might use your BTEC

BTEC Nationals in Business are highly valued by employers. Alternatively, you could progress on to higher education programmes in general business studies, as well as in more specialised areas such as law, human resource management and marketing.

If you decide to enter employment with your BTEC National in Business, a variety of trainee positions exists. Trainee positions may be found in accountancy, retail management, sales, and personnel management. Those who obtain higher qualifications, such as foundation and honours degrees, may move into any of the jobs listed below. This is just a small sample of the sorts of opportunities that could be available:

accountant; advertising account executive; retail, investment or commercial banker; building society manager; industrial or retail buyer; company secretary; commodity or futures broker; distribution or logistics manager; insurance underwriter; management consultant; marketing executive; market research executive; human resources manager; public relations account executive; recruitment consultant; retail manager; sales executive; stockbroker; Business Studies teacher; purchasing manager; owner of your own business.

Skills you need for your sector

Here are some examples of the transferable skills that you could develop on this course. Employers' job vacancy details often refer to them when they advertise for staff. You can mention these skills on your CV to demonstrate the broad range of qualities you have to offer.

Analysing and selecting information

When researching evidence for your assignments, you have to select relevant information to use and make sense of what it is saying. Employers look for these skills in potential employees.

Communicating effectively

Throughout your course, you will develop skills in both written and non-written methods of communication. Employers are always keen to hire good communicators, cutting down on mistakes caused by misunderstandings between different parts of the business.

Teamwork

Much of what goes on in business involves the ability to work well in teams and for teams to work together to solve problems. The BTEC National in Business encourages learners to work together to achieve group and individual goals.

Understanding and interpreting numerical data

Whatever job you perform in a business, there will be occasions when you have to understand and interpret numerical data. This could mean analysing a simple bar chart or line graph, or performing calculations. Again, all employers need people who can demonstrate these skills.

Problem solving

Employers want people who know how to solve problems for themselves and within teams. If employees always rely on their managers to solve problems, the flow of work through the business slows up as a result. Employers want people who show initiative and who can make recommendations for solving problems.

Computer literacy

Increasingly, employers want staff that can use basic and, sometimes, more advanced computer applications. The BTEC National course in Business contains opportunities to practise your IT skills using Word, Excel, the internet and email.

Meeting deadlines

All businesses have objectives that have to be met. In order to meet these objectives, deadlines have to be set at every level of the business. The BTEC National course, with its scheduled programme of assignments, will teach you the importance of meeting deadlines. If you miss assignment deadlines, you run the risk of not achieving the qualification.

Organising your time and prioritisation

Being able to manage your time is critical in the business sector. Sometimes it is difficult to work out which of the many tasks that you have to do is the most important. Sometimes, people try to do too many things at once and are not successful at any of them, causing stress and confusion. Through tutorials, your tutor will help you to manage your time and will assist you in prioritising various tasks.

Writing reports

At some point in your working life, you will probably have to produce a report. Businesses rely on reports to inform people inside and outside the organisation. Your BTEC course will teach you how to structure, write and produce business reports.

Additional skills

In addition to the skills described above, there are a number of other skills that you can develop on the programme. Research has shown that employers also require these additional skills from their staff. **Personal, learning and thinking skills** (PLTS), together with the **functional skills** of English, mathematics and ICT, are essential to success in learning, life and work.

Personal, learning and thinking skills encompass: teamworking; independent enquiry; self-management; reflective learning; effective participation; creative thinking.

These skills enable young people to enter work and engage in adult life as confident, capable individuals. Other skills that good business practitioners might demonstrate are discussed below.

- Working in business will probably require you to **manage resources** (physical and human). A manager in a business must be able to demonstrate good people skills; being able to communicate, guide and motivate others is crucial.

- You will also need to develop your **planning skills**, to enable you to plan ahead and make predictions about what may happen next. Good business managers are able to develop a vision of their business or area of the business in the future. Then they devise strategies to enable this vision to become a reality.

- The world is changing at an accelerating pace and business requires people who can adapt to change. Good managers in business **embrace change** and encourage others to see the benefits to the business of constructive change.

- The ability to be a successful **team member** and **team leader** is something the BTEC National programme strives to develop in learners. As a manager, you will face problems that require you to make decisions and work out solutions. A growing concern is the need for business managers to act ethically, adhering to high personal standards.

Some of the most important attributes a manager must possess include the ability to:

- formulate and stay focused on goals
- allocate resources according to priorities
- make decisions, act upon them and take responsibility.

Step One: Understand your course and how it works

Case study: Understanding the structure of the BTEC National in Business

Zaheer received his GCSE and BTEC First results in the summer. He achieved two grade Cs in English and mathematics, two grade Bs in history and art, and a merit in his BTEC First in Business. He has decided to return to school, where he hopes to enrol on the BTEC National Extended Diploma in Business.

Zaheer has always had a keen interest in business and believes that this qualification will give him a good balance of practice and theory. Zaheer wants to pursue a career in marketing and is attracted by the practical activities and assignments that the BTEC National offers.

'I have discussed in detail with my tutor how the BTEC National Extended Diploma in Business is structured, in particular the units and pathways. The pathways allow you to do more units in a particular specialised area of Business Studies, such as finance. Each unit of the BTEC National in Business has 10 credits. The credit value of a unit is based on the principle that one credit is awarded for the learning outcomes that can be achieved in 10 hours of study.

Over the two years of the programme I will study 18 units, four of which will be mandatory units. This means I have to study 180 credits in total. One mandatory unit will be a marketing unit. Fortunately, the school specialises in marketing and I will be able to choose four other optional marketing units. These four optional units comprise a pathway, and mean that I can get the endorsement 'marketing' in the title of my qualification – BTEC National Extended Diploma in Business (Marketing).

There are other optional units that I think I will also find interesting; I will enjoy the units dealing with finance and accountancy, as I like to work with numbers. I also think the unit on starting a business will be beneficial as it combines all the parts of what I am studying, and will give me a valuable insight into what it takes to start my own business.'

Reflection points

Why do you think it is important for a learner to understand how the BTEC Level 3 National in Business is structured?

Think about what you would do if you were having difficulty understanding the structure of your BTEC Level 3 National in Business.

All BTEC Level 3 National qualifications are **vocational** or **work-related**. This means that you gain specific knowledge and understanding relevant to your chosen area. It gives you several advantages when you start work.

For example, you will already know quite a lot about your chosen area, which will help you settle down more quickly. If you are already employed, you become more valuable to your employer.

Your BTEC course will prepare you for the work you want to do.

There are four types of BTEC Level 3 National qualification:
Certificates, Subsidiary Diplomas, Diplomas and Extended Diplomas

	Certificate	Subsidiary Diploma	Diploma	Extended Diploma
Credit	30	60	120	180
Equivalence	1 AS-level	1 A-level	2 A-levels	3 A-levels

These qualifications are often described as **nested**. This means that they fit inside each other (rather like Russian dolls) because the same units are common to each qualification – so you can progress from one to another easily by completing more units.

TOP TIP

The structure of BTEC Level 3 National qualifications means it's easy to progress from one type to another and gain more credits, as well as specialise in particular areas that interest you.

- Every BTEC Level 3 National qualification has a set number of **mandatory units** that all learners must complete.
- All BTEC Level 3 National qualifications include **optional units** that enable you to study particular areas in more depth.

- Some BTEC Level 3 National qualifications have **specialist pathways**, which may have additional mandatory units. These specialist pathways allow you to follow your career aims more precisely. For example, if you are studying to become an IT practitioner, you can choose pathways in Software Development, Networking, Systems Support or IT and Business.

- On all BTEC courses you are expected to be responsible for your own learning. Obviously your tutor will give you help and guidance when necessary but you also need to be 'self-starting' and able to use your own initiative. Ideally, you can also assess how well you are doing and make improvements when necessary.

- BTEC Level 3 National grades convert to UCAS points, just like A-levels, but the way you are assessed and graded on a BTEC course is different, as you will see in the next section.

Key points

- You can study part-time or full-time for your BTEC Level 3 National.

- You can do a Certificate, Subsidiary Diploma, Diploma, or Extended Diploma, and progress easily from one to the other.

- You will study both mandatory units and optional units on your course.

- When you have completed your BTEC course you can get a job (or **apprenticeship**), use your qualification to develop your career and/or continue studying to degree level.

- On all BTEC Level 3 National courses, the majority of your learning is practical and vocationally focused to develop the skills you need for your chosen career.

Using the Edexcel website to find out about your course

- You can check all the details about your BTEC Level 3 National course on the Edexcel website – go to www.edexcel.com.

- Enter the title of your BTEC Level 3 National qualification in the qualifications finder.

- Now find the specification in the list of documents. This is a long document so don't try to print it. Instead, look at the information on the units you will be studying to see the main topics you will cover.

- Then save the document or bookmark the page so that you can easily refer to it again if you need to.

Action points

1   By discussing with your tutor and by exploring the Edexcel website, find out the key information about your course and use it to complete the 'Important Information' form on the next page. You can refer to this form at any time to refresh your memory about any part of your studies.

a) Check whether you are studying for a BTEC Level 3 Certificate, Subsidiary Diploma, Diploma, or Extended Diploma and the number of units you will be studying.

b) Find out the titles of the mandatory units you will be studying.

c) Find out the titles of the optional units and identify the ones offered at your centre.

d) Check the length of your course, and when you will be studying each unit.

e) Identify the optional units you will be taking. On some National courses you will do this at the start, while on others you may make your final decision later.

f) Find out other relevant information about your BTEC Level 3 National qualification. Your centre may have already given you details about the structure.

g) Ask your tutor to help you to complete point 10 on the form. Depending on your course, you may be developing specific additional or personal skills – such as personal, learning and thinking skills (PLTS) and functional skills – or spending time on work experience, going on visits or doing other activities linked to your subject area.

h) Talk to your tutor about point 12 on the form as your sources of information will depend on the careers guidance and information at your centre. You may find it useful to exchange ideas with other members of your class.

	IMPORTANT INFORMATION ON MY BTEC LEVEL 3 NATIONAL COURSE
1	The title of the BTEC Level 3 National qualification I am studying is:
2	The length of my course is:
3	The total number of units I will study is:
4	The number of mandatory units I have to study is:
5	The titles of these mandatory units and the dates (or terms) when I will study them are:
6	The main topics I will learn in each mandatory unit include:

	IMPORTANT INFORMATION ON MY BTEC LEVEL 3 NATIONAL COURSE
7	The number of optional units I have to study is:
8	The titles of the optional units I will study are:
9	The main topics I will learn in each optional unit include:
10	Other important aspects of my course are:
11	After I have achieved my BTEC Level 3 National my options include:
12	Useful sources of information I can use to find out more about these options include:

2 Many learners already have information, contacts or direct experiences that relate to their course. For example, you may have a specific interest or hobby that links to a unit, such as being a St John Ambulance cadet if you are studying Public Services. Think about the relevant sources of information you already have access to and complete the table below.

MY INFORMATION SOURCES	
Experts I know	(Who they are, what they know)
My hobbies and interests	(What they are, what they involve)
My job(s)	(Past and present work and work experience, and what I did)
Programmes I like to watch	(What these are, how they relate to my course)
Magazines and/or books I read	(What these are, examples of relevant articles)
ICT sources	(My centre's intranet as well as useful websites)
Other	(Other sources relevant for my particular course and the topics I will be studying)

Part-time jobs can help you to understand how businesses operate.

Activity: Your future options

At the beginning of a new course it is helpful to think about what options may be available to you for your career pathway in the business sector. All assignments on the programme contribute to your final grade and knowing what you are aiming for will help to keep you motivated.

Using a mind map to explore different ideas is a good way to consider the range of options available to you. You will also be able to find out the requirements for each career pathway. For example, if you wish to work in finance, you could explore the different routes to becoming an accountant.

You will find the internet a useful source of information. A good starting point is the Monster Job Search website. Go to page 92 to find out how to access the website.

Create a mind map on the next page to record your ideas.

TOP TIP

People usually perform better if they understand why they have chosen, or been asked, to do something.

Career options available to me in Business

Step Two: Understand how you are assessed and graded

Case study: Assessment and grading

During Harris's course induction for the BTEC National Extended Diploma in Business, the tutor spends a lot of time ensuring that the learners understand how they are to be assessed and graded, how unit points combine to give an overall grade, and how the qualification grades convert into UCAS points.

'My induction week has been great as it has allowed me to get to know other learners on my course. We've also spent a lot of time discussing how we are to be assessed for each unit. The tutor explained to us that assignments take a variety of forms, including presentations, written assignments and reports. There are no examinations on the BTEC National Extended Diploma in Business, but we found out how we will be graded at pass, merit or distinction level.

The tutor clarified for us how the command words used in the performance criteria dictate whether a criterion is at pass, merit or distinction level. Criteria at pass level usually ask you to identify or describe, while those at merit or distinction level require a more in-depth answer and often use command words such as analyse or evaluate. We have to achieve at least all the pass criteria for an individual unit to pass that unit.

When I finish this qualification, I will have attained the equivalent of three A-levels and, hopefully, will be able to progress onto a marketing degree at university. The qualifications carry the same UCAS points as A-levels and my overall grade for the qualification will be calculated using a unit point system – my score for each unit will be added up to obtain an overall grade.

I am glad that I have had the chance to understand the methods of assessment, grading, and the unit points system; this will all be a huge help to me once I get going on the course. I can't wait to get started now.'

Reflection points

How well do you think the BTEC National Extended Diploma in Business will prepare Harris for higher education?

A learner is aiming for a distinction grade in the BTEC Level 3 National in Business. Think about the key factors they will need to consider in order to achieve this goal.

Your assessment

This section looks at the importance of your assignments, how they are graded and how this converts into unit points and UCAS points. Unlike A-levels, there are no externally-set final exams on a BTEC course. Even if you know this because you already have a BTEC First qualification, you should still read this section as now you will be working at a different level.

Your learning is assessed by **assignments**, set by your tutors. You will complete these throughout your course, using many different **assessment methods**, such as real-life case studies, **projects** and presentations. Some assignments may be work-based or **time-constrained** – it depends very much on the vocational area you are studying.

Your assignments are based on **learning outcomes** set by Edexcel. These are listed for each unit in your course specification. You must achieve **all** the learning outcomes to pass each unit.

Important skills to help you achieve your grades include:

- researching and analysing information (see page 59)
- using your time effectively (see page 25)
- working co-operatively as a member of a team (see page 53).

Your grades, unit points and UCAS points

On a BTEC Level 3 National course, assessments that meet the learning outcomes are graded as pass, merit or distinction. The different grades within each unit are set out by Edexcel as **grading criteria** in a **grading grid**. These criteria identify the **higher-level skills** you must demonstrate

to achieve a higher grade (see also Step Six – Understand your assessment, on page 35).

All your assessment grades earn **unit points**. The total points you get for all your units determines your final qualification grade(s) – pass, merit or distinction. You get:

- one final grade if you are taking a Certificate or Subsidiary Diploma
- two final grades if you are taking a Diploma
- three final grades if you are taking an Extended Diploma.

Your points and overall grade(s) convert to **UCAS points**, which you need to be accepted onto a degree course. For example, if you achieve three final pass grades for your BTEC Level 3 Extended Diploma, you get 120 UCAS Tariff points. If you achieve three final distinction grades, this increases to 360 – equivalent to three GCE A-levels.

Please note that all UCAS information was correct at the time of going to print. However, we would advise that you check their website for the most up to date information. See page 92 for how to access their website.

 Case study: Securing a university place

Chris and Shaheeda both want a university place and have worked hard on their BTEC Level 3 Extended Diploma course.

Chris's final score is 226 unit points, which converts to 280 UCAS Tariff points. Shaheeda has a total score of 228 unit points – just two points more – which converts to 320 UCAS points! This is because a score of between 204

and 227 unit points gives 280 UCAS points, whereas a score of 228 to 251 points gives 320 UCAS points.

Shaheeda is delighted because this increases her chances of getting a place on the degree course she wants. Chris is annoyed. He says if he had realised he would have worked harder on his last assignment to get two points more.

You start to earn points from your first assessment, so you get many benefits from settling in quickly and doing good work from the start. Understanding how **grade boundaries** work also helps you to focus your efforts to get the best possible final grade.

You will be able to discuss your learning experiences, your personal progress and the

achievement of your learning objectives in **individual tutorials** with your tutor. These enable you to monitor your progress and overcome temporary difficulties. You can also talk about any worries you have. Your tutor is one of your most important resources and a tutorial gives you their undivided attention.

You can talk through any questions or problems in your tutorials.

Key points

- Your learning is assessed in a variety of ways, such as by assignments, projects and real-life case studies.

- You need to demonstrate specific knowledge and skills to achieve the learning outcomes set by Edexcel. You must achieve all the grading criteria to pass a unit.

- The grading criteria for pass, merit and distinction are shown in a grading grid for the unit. Higher-level skills are needed for higher grades.

- The assessment grades of pass, merit and distinction convert to unit points. The total unit points you receive for the course determines your final overall grade(s) and UCAS points.

TOP TIP

It's always tempting to spend longer on work you like doing and are good at, but focusing on improving your weak areas will do more to boost your overall grade(s).

Action points

1 Find out more about your own course by carrying out this activity.

a) Find the learning outcomes for the units you are currently studying. Your tutor may have given you these, or you can find them in your course specification – go to www.edexcel.com.

b) Look at the grading grid for the units and identify the way the requirements change for the higher grades. If there are some unfamiliar words, check these in Step Six of this guide (see page 35 onwards).

c) If the unit points system still seems complicated, ask your tutor to explain it.

d) Check the UCAS points you would need for the course or university which interests you.

e) Design a form you can use to record the unit points you earn throughout your course. Keep this up-to-date. Regularly check how your points relate to your overall grade(s), based on the grade boundaries for your qualification. Your tutor can give you this information or you can check it yourself in the course specification.

Activity: Understanding how you are assessed and graded

To see how well you have grasped the main issues concerning assessment and grading on the BTEC National in Business, try to answer the following questions about the qualification.

How many different types of assessment method can you think of?

What are the four learning outcomes for Unit 1: The Business Environment?

Why do you think it is important to understand fully how your BTEC course is structured, how you are assessed and graded, and what the possible progression routes are?

Having read through this section on understanding how you are assessed and graded, list any areas that you feel are not quite clear. Make a point of discussing these with your tutor to resolve any issues.

Step Three: Understand yourself

Case study: Becoming self-aware

When Amber starts her BTEC National Diploma in Business, she is lacking in confidence and tends to have a negative attitude towards new challenges. She discusses these feelings with her tutor, who introduces her to an unfamiliar term; Amber's tutor tells her that she needs to become more 'self-aware'.

Self-awareness is helpful to us throughout our lives, and the ability to self-reflect is particularly useful in an educational environment. In simple terms, self-awareness is about trying to understand who we really are and why we do the things we do, in the way we do them. By becoming a bit more self-aware, we can gain a greater degree of control over how we operate in the present, instead of reacting in a way that is conditioned by our past.

Amber thinks about this concept and about her own personality, which she has already assessed during her induction to the programme. She is a quiet, reserved person who likes working independently. Amber realises that she needs to take greater control of her life and where it is heading, to be more positive and to become more decisive. She thinks this will help her get more out of life. She also realises that there are a number of skills she needs to work on, such as her teamworking and research skills.

Amber works hard at becoming more self-aware and takes a number of steps to help her on this journey.

- First, she decides to talk to friends and other people whose opinions she values, asking them about her strengths and weaknesses.
- Then she makes a list of her strengths and weaknesses. She believes that the more she knows about her weaknesses, the better chance she has of turning these into strengths.
- Another method she finds useful is to imagine herself dealing with situations she hasn't faced before, and she reflects on her responses to real situations.
- Amber also thinks about her body language and other subtle messages she sends out in her everyday life. She is aware of how others may view these cues, and is determined to send out more positive signals.

Over time, Amber is becoming more self-aware and many of the strategies described here have helped her to achieve this goal. Becoming more self-aware has allowed her to change her behaviour for the better.

Reflection points

What do you think is meant by the term 'self-awareness'?

Why is there a link between Amber's personality and becoming more self-aware?

Think about how Amber's skills set and abilities might be improved by increased self-awareness.

Self-awareness means understanding how you 'tick'. For example, do you prefer practical activities rather than theory? Do you prefer to draw or sketch an idea, rather than write about it?

Self-awareness is important as it makes you less reliant on other people's opinions and gives you confidence in your own judgement. You can also reflect on your actions to learn from your experiences.

Self-awareness also means knowing your own strengths and weaknesses. Knowing your strengths enables you to feel positive and confident about yourself and your abilities. Knowing your weaknesses means you know the areas you need to develop.

You can analyse yourself by looking at...

... your personality and preferences

You may have taken a personality test at your centre. If not, your tutor may recommend one to use, or there are many available online.

Many employers ask job candidates to complete a personality test so that they can match the type of work they are offering to the most suitable candidates. Although these tests can only give a broad indication of someone's personality they may help to avoid mismatches, such as hiring someone who is introverted to work in sales.

... your skills and abilities

To succeed in your assignments, and to progress in a career, requires a number of skills. Some may be vocationally specific, or professional, skills that you can improve during your course – such as sporting performance on a Sports course. Others are broader skills that are invaluable no matter what you are studying – such as communicating clearly and co-operating with others.

You will work faster and more accurately, and have greater confidence, if you are skilled and proficient. A quick skills check will identify any problem areas.

TOP TIP

Use the Skills Building section on page 81 to identify the skills you need for your course. You'll also find hints and tips for improving any weak areas.

Key points

- You need certain skills and abilities to get the most out of your BTEC Level 3 National course and to develop your career potential.
- Knowing your strengths and weaknesses is a sign of maturity. It gives you greater confidence in your abilities and enables you to focus on areas for improvement.

TOP TIP

You will find more help on developing your skills and abilities in the sections on: Working as a member of a group; Using time wisely; Researching and analysing information; and Making effective presentations.

Action points

1 Gain insight into your own personality by answering each of the following statements **True** or **False** with a tick. Be honest!

		True	False
a)	If someone annoys me, I can tell them about it without causing offence.		
b)	If someone is talking, I often interrupt them to give them my opinion.		
c)	I get really stressed if I'm under pressure.		
d)	I can sometimes become very emotional and upset on other people's behalf.		
e)	I sometimes worry that I can't cope and may make a mess of something.		
f)	I am usually keen, enthusiastic and motivated to do well.		
g)	I enjoy planning and organising my work.		
h)	I find it easy to work and co-operate with other people and take account of their opinions.		
i)	I am easily influenced by other people.		
j)	I often jump to conclusions and judge people and situations on first impressions.		
k)	I prefer to rely on facts and experience rather than following my instincts.		

Now identify which of the skills and qualities in the box below will be really important in your chosen career.

> tact   truthfulness   listening skills
>
> **staying calm under pressure**
>
> **empathy with others   self-confidence**
>
> **initiative   planning and organising**
>
> **working with others   self-assurance**
>
> **objective judgements**

Use your answers to identify areas you should work on to be successful in the future.

2 As part of the UCAS process, all **higher education** applicants have to write a personal statement. This is different from a CV, which is a summary of achievements that all job applicants prepare. You may have already prepared a CV but not thought about a personal statement. Now is your chance to!

Read the information about personal statement in the box. Then answer these questions:

a) Explain why personal statements are so important for higher education applicants.

b) Why do you think it is important for your personal statement to read well and be error-free?

c) Suggest three reasons why you shouldn't copy a pre-written statement you have found online.

d) Check the websites you can access from the hotlink given in the box to see what to include in the statement and how to set it out.

e) Prepare a bullet point list of ten personal facts. Focus on your strengths and good reasons why you should be given a place on the higher education course of your choice. If possible, discuss your list with your tutor. Then keep it safely, as it will be useful if you need to write a personal statement later.

Personal statements

This is the information that all higher education applicants have to put in the blank space on their UCAS form. The aim is to sell yourself to admissions tutors. It can be pretty scary, especially if you haven't written anything like it before.

So, where do you start?

First, **never** copy pre-written statements you find online. These are just for guidance. Even worse are websites that offer to write your statement for a fee, and send you a few general, pre-written paragraphs. Forget them all: you can do better!

Imagine you are an admissions tutor with 60 places to offer to 200 applicants. What will you need to read in a personal statement to persuade you to offer the applicant a place?

Most likely, clear explanations about:

- what the applicant can contribute to the course
- why the applicant really wants a place on your course
- what the applicant has done to further his/her own interests in this area, eg voluntary work
- attributes that show this applicant would be a definite bonus – such as innovative ideas, with evidence eg 'I organised a newsletter which we published every three months …'

A personal statement should be well written, with no grammatical or spelling errors and organised into clear paragraphs.

There are a number of helpful websites. Go to page 92 to find out how to access them.

Activity: UCAS personal statement

The box contains a UCAS personal statement from a learner who wants to apply for a Business course at a higher education institute. Read the extract and answer the questions that follow.

I have always wanted to study at university and get a job that will allow me to taste the highlife, staying in posh hotels and travelling around the world. My father runs a small business and often talks about his business ventures; this has rubbed off on me. I am excited by the 'dog-eat-dog' ruthless world of business.

By the time I began my GCSE year, I knew that I wanted to do a Business and Management degree course. I felt a lot of it would come naturally to me, remembering all the advice I had heard from my father. It is satisfying to know that I would use hardly anything I had learnt in school when studying business. One of the most interesting aspects of business for me is international markets and economics. I regularly go camping and recently hitchhiked across Europe with a friend.

Over the course of the BTEC National, I have done a lot of presenting and I am now very skilled in this area. I have been appointed to the role of prefect, I am a member of the student council in my school, and I also lend a hand in managing and working in our school shop, which have all helped me in my studies.

I have a large number of hobbies, but my main interest is in computers and, in particular, computer games. I always assist my family and friends with technical problems. I learnt how to build a computer from scratch, and have modified individual components. I find computers extremely satisfying as there is always going to be a problem, and therefore a solution, which may not always be obvious.

I play a lot of sport and play for the school football team. I also like swimming and reading.

1 What is wrong with the first paragraph?

2 Do you think the learner has given enough information on how they have developed their knowledge of business studies?

3 Do you think the learner has adequately described his or her extracurricular activities and career aspirations?

4 Overall, how would you evaluate this personal statement? Give reasons for your views.

Step Four: Use your time wisely

Case study: Organisation, planning and time management

When she first started the BTEC National Diploma in Business, Leona was very disorganised. Her loose notes were always crammed into her bag and she never filed anything, even though her parents had bought her some ringbinders for this purpose. Starting work on her first assignment, Leona began to panic as she could not find any of the notes or handouts that she needed. Her electronic organisation was no better, as she could never remember where she had saved important pieces of information on the computer. Leona went to see her tutor about the problem.

'I sat down with my tutor, one to one, and he reminded me of what we had learnt in the induction programme about how important it is to be organised, to plan and to think ahead. He advised me to devise a system for filing my notes and handouts, and to plan using timelines to ensure that my work is always completed on time. Similarly, with stored information on the computer, the tutor suggested that I try to save things into clearly identified files, so that I can retrieve the information easily later on.

It took a lot of practice to change my habits but, with perseverance, I am now far more organised. I even tidy up my bedroom regularly, so I don't go into a mad panic when I need to find something.'

Leona has just started a work placement at a busy office that processes sales invoices. On her first day, she attends a compulsory half-day training course on time management. All new starters at the company have to attend this course as the firm is deadline-driven; it is vital that staff remain focused on achieving their individual and department targets.

The work experience time management course teaches Leona how to prioritise tasks – how to decide which tasks have to be completed immediately and which ones can be left until later. Leona enjoys the course and it reinforces what she has learnt on the BTEC National Diploma in Business about time management and planning.

On returning to school after her work experience, Leona now understands that good organisation, planning and time management aren't just skills that she needs to use to meet her deadlines for her Diploma assignments; these are important skills for working in business, and for life in general.

Reflection points

What do you think this case study reveals about the benefits of planning and being organised?

Think about the approach you currently take to your studies. How good are you at:

- planning your time effectively
- setting yourself targets
- prioritising tasks
- monitoring your progress?

If you need to make improvements in some or all of these areas, how would you go about doing this?

Most learners have to combine course commitments with other responsibilities such as a job (either full- or part-time) and family responsibilities. You will also want to see your friends and keep up your hobbies and interests. Juggling these successfully means you need to be able to use your time wisely.

This involves planning what to do and when to do it to prevent panics about unexpected deadlines. As your course progresses, this becomes even more important as your workload may increase towards the end of a term. In some cases there could be two or more assignments to complete simultaneously. Although tutors try to avoid clashes of this sort, it is sometimes inevitable.

To cope successfully, you need time-management skills, in particular:

- how to organise your time to be more productive
- how to prioritise tasks
- how to overcome time-wasters.

Organising your time

- **Use a diary or wall chart.**
  Using a different colour pen for each, enter:
  - your course commitments, eg assignment dates, tutorials, visits
  - important personal commitments, eg sports matches, family birthdays
  - your work commitments.

TOP TIP

A diary is useful because you can update it as you go, but a wall chart gives you a better overview of your commitments over several weeks. Keep your diary or chart up-to-date and check ahead regularly so that you have prior warning of important dates.

- **Identify how you currently use your time.**
  - Work out how much time you spend at your centre, at work, at home and on social activities.
  - Identify which commitments are vital and which are optional so you can find extra time if necessary.
- **Plan and schedule future commitments.**
  - Write down any appointments and tasks you must do.
  - Enter assignment review dates and final deadline dates in different colours.

- This should stop you from arranging a dental appointment on the same morning that you are due to give an important presentation – or planning a hectic social life when you have lots of course work to do.
- **Decide your best times for doing course work.**
  - Expect to do most of your course work in your own time.
  - Work at the time of day when you feel at your best.
  - Work regularly, and in relatively short bursts, rather than once or twice a week for very long stretches.
  - If you're a night owl, allow an hour to 'switch off' before you go to bed.
- **Decide where to work.**
  - Choose somewhere you can concentrate without interruption.
  - Make sure there is space for resources you use, such as books or specialist equipment.
  - You also need good lighting and a good – but not too comfortable – chair.
  - If you can't find suitable space at home, check out your local or college library.
- **Assemble the items you need.**
  - Book ahead to get specific books, journals or DVDs from the library.
  - Ensure you have your notes, handouts and assignment brief with you.
  - Use sticky notes to mark important pages in textbooks or folders.

TOP TIP

Set yourself a target when you start work, so that you feel positive and productive at the end. Always try to end a session when a task is going well, rather than when you are stuck. Then you will be keener to go back to it the next day. Note down outstanding tasks you need to continue with next time.

- **Plan ahead**
  - If anything is unclear about an assignment, ask your tutor for an explanation as soon as you can.
  - Break down long tasks or assignments into manageable chunks, eg find information, decide what to use, create a plan for finished work, write rough draft of first section, etc.
  - Work back from deadline dates so that you allow plenty of time to do the work.
  - Always allow more time than you need. It is better to finish early than to run out of time.

TOP TIP

If you are working on a task as a group, organise and agree times to work together. Make sure you have somewhere to meet where you can work without disturbing other courses or groups.

- **Be self-disciplined.**
  - Don't put things off because you're not in the mood. Make it easier by doing simple tasks first to get a sense of achievement. Then move on to something harder.
  - Plan regular breaks. If you're working hard you need a change of activity to recharge your batteries.
  - If you have a serious problem or personal crisis, talk to your personal tutor promptly.

TOP TIP

Make sure you know the consequences of missing an assignment deadline, as well as the dispensations and exemptions that can be given if you have an unavoidable and serious problem, such as illness (see also pages 78–80).

How to prioritise tasks

Prioritising means doing the most important and urgent task first. Normally this will be the task or assignment with the closest deadline or the one that will most affect your overall course grades.

One way of prioritising is to group tasks into ABC categories.

Category A tasks	These must be done now as they are very important and cannot be delayed, eg completing an assignment to be handed in tomorrow.
Category B tasks	These are jobs you should do if you have time, because otherwise they will rapidly become Category A, eg getting a book that you need for your next assignment.
Category C tasks	These are tasks you should do if you have the time, eg rewriting notes jotted down quickly in a lesson.

Expect to be flexible. For example, if you need to allow time for information to arrive, then send for this first. If you are working in a team, take into account other people's schedules when you are making arrangements.

Avoiding time-wasters

Everyone has days when they don't know where the time has gone. It may be because they were constantly interrupted or because things just kept going wrong. Whatever the reason, the end result is that some jobs don't get done.

If this happens to you regularly, you need to take steps to keep on track.

Some useful tips are:

- **Warn people in advance when you will be working.**

  – Ask them to not interrupt you.

  – If you are in a separate room, shut the door. If someone comes in, make it clear you don't want to talk.

  – If that doesn't work, find somewhere else (or some other time) to work.

- **Switch off your mobile, TV, radio and iPod/ MP3 player.**

  – Don't respond to, or make, calls or texts.

  – If someone rings your home phone, let voicemail answer or ask them to call back later.

- **Be strict with yourself when you are working online.**

  – Don't check your email until you've finished work.

  – Don't get distracted when searching for information.

  – Keep away from social networking sites.

- **Avoid displacement activities.**

  – These are the normally tedious jobs, such as cleaning your computer screen, that suddenly seem far more attractive than working!

TOP TIP

Benefits to managing your own time include being less stressed (because you are not reacting to problems or crises), producing better work and having time for a social life.

Talking to friends can occupy a lot of time.

TOP TIP

The first step in managing your own time is learning to say 'no' (nicely!) if someone asks you to do something tempting when you should be working.

Key points

- Being in control of your time allows you to balance your commitments according to their importance and means you won't let anyone down.

- Organising yourself and your time involves knowing how you spend your time now, planning when and where it is best to work, scheduling commitments and setting sensible timescales to complete your work.

- Knowing how to prioritise means you will schedule work effectively according to its urgency and importance. You will need self-discipline to follow the schedule you have set for yourself.

- Identifying ways in which you may waste time means you can guard against these to achieve your goals more easily.

Action points

1 Start planning your time properly.

a) Find out how many assignments you will have this term, and when you will get them. Put this information into your diary or planner.

b) Update this with your other commitments for the term – both work/course-related and social. Identify possible clashes and decide how to resolve the problem.

c) Identify one major task or assignment you will do soon. Divide it into manageable chunks and decide how long to allow for each chunk, plus some spare time for any problems. If possible, check your ideas with your tutor before you put them into your planner.

2 How good are you at being responsible for your own learning?

a) Fill in the following table. Score yourself out of 5 for each area: where 0 is awful and 5 is excellent. Ask a friend or relative to score you as well. See if you can explain any differences.

	Scoring yourself	Other person's score for you
Being punctual		
Organisational ability		
Tidiness		
Working accurately		
Finding and correcting own mistakes		
Solving problems		
Accepting responsibility		
Working with details		
Planning how to do a job		
Using own initiative		
Thinking up new ideas		
Meeting deadlines		

b) Draw up your own action plan for areas where you need to improve. If possible, talk this through at your next **tutorial**.

TOP TIP

Don't waste time doing things that distract you when studying for this course. In business, time costs money.

Activity: Prioritising tasks, eliminating time wasters

In the previous case study (see page 25), Leona was taking part in a work placement after attending a time management course. She was given a number of tasks to complete during the two-week period of her work experience.

The tasks were as follows:

1 Send a thank you letter to a customer who has written to the company praising the standard of service that she experienced.

2 Produce a report for the department manager on whether targets have been achieved over the last month. The departmental manager has to present this report to senior managers the day after tomorrow.

3 Send an email to other staff giving them details about the Christmas lunch that will take place in December (four months away).

4 Phone a customer who gives the firm a lot of business but who is threatening to take her business elsewhere unless she receives a satisfactory explanation as to why her invoices were three days late last month.

Leona remembered what she had learnt about time management and decided to prioritise the tasks and to plan her workload. Of the four key tasks that Leona was asked to complete, which do you think were her first, second, third and fourth priority? Give reasons for your selections.

Explain why the key to successful time management is planning.

If you were Leona, what measures would you take to organise your time?

Step Five: Utilise all your resources

Case study: Identifying resources

David is a junior marketing executive with a large frozen food company. His line manager has asked David to investigate whether the business should launch a new frozen pizza aimed at customers who are under 25 years old. David starts by listing all of the resources that may assist him in this investigation.

- The company has its own team of interviewers, who can be called on to undertake any research.
- David has access to some recent market research reports, containing information on trends in the frozen pizza market.
- The company has a database containing the names and addresses of over 2500 under-25 year olds who have previously taken part in market research.
- He also has at his disposal information from the National Statistical Office about the current state of the frozen pizza market.
- Another member of the marketing team has recently conducted a similar research project on frozen desserts.

Reflection points

What do you think is meant by the term 'resource'?

The case study gives some examples of resources that David could use in his investigation. Can you think of any other resources that he could use?

Why do you think it is important to identify your resources before you embark on a project?

Think about the materials and equipment you will need when you start your BTEC Level 3 National in Business. Make a list.

Your resources are all the things that can help you to be successful in your BTEC Level 3 National qualification, from your favourite website to your study buddy (see page 32) who collects handouts for you if you miss a class.

Your centre will provide essential resources, such as a library with appropriate books and electronic reference sources, the computer network and internet access. You will have to provide basic resources such as pens, pencils and file folders yourself. If you have to buy your own textbooks, look after them carefully so you can sell them on at the end of your course.

Here is a list of resources, with tips for getting the best out of them.

- **Course information**. This includes your course specification, this Study Skills Guide and all information on the Edexcel website relating to your BTEC Level 3 National course. Course information from your centre will include term dates, assignment dates and your timetable. Keep everything safely so you can refer to it whenever you need to clarify something.

- **Course materials**. These include course handouts, printouts, your own notes and textbooks. Put handouts into an A4 folder as soon as you get them. Use a separate folder for each unit you study.

TOP TIP

Filing notes and handouts promptly means they don't get lost, will stay clean and uncrumpled and you won't waste time looking for them.

- **Stationery**. You need pens and pencils, a notepad, a hole puncher, a stapler and sets of dividers. Dividers should be clearly labelled to help you store and quickly find notes, printouts and handouts. Your notes should be headed and dated, and those from your own research must also include your source (see Step Eight – page 59 onwards.)

- **People**. Your tutors, specialist staff at college, classmates, your employer and work colleagues, your relatives and friends are all valuable resources. Many will have particular skills or work in the vocational area that you are studying. Talking to other learners can help to clarify issues that there may not have been time to discuss fully in class.

A **study buddy** is another useful resource as they can make notes and collect handouts if you miss a session. (Remember to return the favour when they are away.)

Always be polite when you are asking people for information. Prepare the questions first and remember that you are asking for help, not trying to get them to do the work for you! If you are interviewing someone for an assignment or project, good preparations are vital. (See Step Eight – page 59 onwards.)

If someone who did the course before you offers help, be careful. It is likely the course requirements will have changed. Never be tempted to copy their assignments (or someone else's). This is **plagiarism** – a deadly sin in the educational world (see also Step Six – page 36).

TOP TIP

A positive attitude, an enquiring mind and the ability to focus on what is important will have a major impact on your final result.

Key points

- Resources help you to achieve your qualification. Find out what resources you have available to you and use them wisely.
- Have your own stationery items.
- Know how to use central facilities and resources such as the library, learning resource centres and your computer network. Always keep to the policy on IT use in your centre.
- People are a key resource – school or college staff, work colleagues, members of your class, friends, family and people who are experts in their field.

Action points

1 **a)** List the resources you will need to complete your course successfully. Identify which ones will be provided by your school or college, and which you need to supply yourself.

   b) Go through your list again and identify the resources you already have (or know how to access) and those you don't.

   c) Compare your list with a friend's and decide how to obtain and access the resources you need. Add any items to your list that you forgot.

   d) List the items you still need to get and set a target date for doing this.

2 'Study buddy' schemes operate in many centres. Find out if this applies to your own centre and how you can make the best use of it.

   In some you can choose your study buddy, in others people are paired up by their tutor.
   - Being a study buddy might mean just collecting handouts when the other person is absent, and giving them important news.
   - It may also mean studying together and meeting (or keeping contact by phone or email) to exchange ideas and share resources.

With a study buddy you can share resources and stay on top of the course if you're ever away.

Activity: Using resources

You will use various resources as you study on the BTEC National in Business, and these will differ depending on the activity or assignment you are working on.

Consider an assignment that asks you to investigate market research carried out by a company. You have decided to approach a local toy manufacturer because a member of your family works there in the administration department. Your contact has given you the names of the market research manager and two other members of her staff. They have indicated that they are happy to give you information about the market research undertaken by the company, as long as it does not breach confidentiality rules.

Before visiting these people, you read through your course notes on market research to ensure you are familiar with the terms and processes involved. Some of your course notes were given to you by your study buddy after you were off with flu. You also refer to the course specification to ensure that you will be able to cover the learning outcomes for this assignment.

Name a people resource that will be important in this assignment.

What course material may be useful for this assignment?

Describe the key advantages of introducing a 'study buddy' scheme in your centre.

Step Six: Understand your assessment

Case study: Preparing for assignment success

Zara has just received her first assignment and is pleased to see that it is about the ownership of businesses, a topic she finds interesting. She is keen and decides to start her assignment that evening. She begins by researching business ownership, making notes as she goes. She is soon ready to start writing about the various types of business ownership that exist. However, she doesn't read the assignment instructions or questions before commencing.

Zara describes every type of ownership and finds that, by doing this, she fills up eight sides of paper – this seems like enough for the entire assignment. She is really pleased with the way the assignment is going and feels that it is nearly finished, so she decides there is no rush to get on with it. Zara doesn't return to the assignment for two weeks.

A friend mentions that the assignment is due in the next day, so Zara spends that evening tidying up her work. She thinks that the work she has done will gain her a good grade. She submits her work and, one week later, she has a tutorial with her tutor who tells her that she has not produced the evidence to obtain even a pass grade. This comes as complete shock to Zara.

Reflection points

Describe the key mistake that you think Zara made.

Why do you think it is very important to read the assignment brief a number of times and to be clear about what is required?

If Zara had read the instructions but was still unsure how to proceed, what should she have done?

Zara completed her assignment by describing different types of ownership. Some of the questions in the assignment (which she hadn't read properly) asked her to explain and evaluate various aspects of ownership. What do you think are the differences between the command words **describe**, **explain** and **evaluate**?

Being successful on any BTEC Level 3 National course means first understanding what you must do in your assignments – and then doing it.

Your assignments focus on topics you have already covered in class. If you've attended regularly, you should be able to complete them confidently.

However, there are some common pitfalls it's worth thinking about. Here are tips to avoid them:

- Read the instructions (the assignment brief) properly and several times before you start.

- Make sure you understand what you are supposed to do. Ask if anything is unclear.

- Complete every part of a task. If you ignore a question, you can't meet the grading criteria.

- Prepare properly. Do your research or reading before you start. Don't guess the answers.

- Communicate your ideas clearly. You can check this by asking someone who doesn't know the subject to look at your work.

- Only include relevant information. Padding out answers makes it look as if you don't know your subject.

- Do the work earlier rather than later to avoid any last-minute panics.

- Pay attention to advice and feedback that your tutor has given you.

The assignment 'brief'

This may be longer than its name implies! The assignment brief includes all the instructions for an assignment and several other details, as you can see in the table below.

What will you find in a BTEC Level 3 National assignment brief?	
Content	Details
Title	This will link to the unit and learning outcomes
Format/style	Written assignment, presentation, demonstration, etc
Preparation	Read case study, do research, etc
Learning outcomes	These state the knowledge you must demonstrate to obtain a required grade
Grading criterion/ criteria covered	eg P1/M1/D1
Individual/group work	Remember to identify your own contribution in any group work
Feedback	Tutor, peer review
Interim review dates	Dates to see your tutor
Final deadline	Last submission date

Your centre's rules and regulations

Your centre will have several policies and guidelines about assignments, which you need to check carefully. Many, such as those listed below, relate to Edexcel policies and guidelines.

- The procedure to follow if you have a serious problem and can't meet a deadline. An extension may be granted.
- The penalty for missing a deadline without good reason.
- The penalty for copying someone else's work. This is usually severe, so never share your work (or CDs or USB flash drive) with anyone else, and don't borrow theirs.
- **Plagiarism** is also serious misconduct. This means copying someone's work (see also page 32) or quoting from books and websites and pretending it is your own work.
- The procedure to follow if you disagree with the grade you are given.

Understanding the question or task

There are two aspects to a question or task. The first is the **command words**, which are described below. The second is the **presentation instructions**, which is what you are asked to do – don't write a report when you should be producing a chart!

Command words, such as 'explain', 'describe', 'analyse' and 'evaluate' state how a question must be answered. You may be asked to 'describe' something at pass level, but you will need to do more, perhaps 'analyse' or 'evaluate', to achieve merit or distinction.

Many learners fail to achieve higher grades because they don't realise the difference between these words. Instead of analysing or evaluating they give an explanation instead. Adding more details won't achieve a higher grade – you need to change your whole approach to the answer.

The **grading grid** for each unit of your course gives you the command words, so that you know what to do to achieve a pass, merit or distinction. The tables that follow show you what is usually required when you see a particular command word. These are just examples to guide you as the exact response will depend on the question. If you have any doubts, check with your tutor before you start work.

There are two important points to note.

- A command word, such as 'create' or 'explain' may be repeated in the grading criteria for different grades. In these cases the complexity or range of the task itself increases at the higher grades.
- Command words vary depending on your vocational area. So Art and Design grading

grids may use different command words from Applied Science, for example.

TOP TIP

Look at this section again when you get your first assignment and check the command words against these explanations.

To obtain a pass grade

To achieve a pass you must usually demonstrate that you understand the important facts relating to a topic and can state these clearly and concisely.

Command words for a pass	Meaning
Create (or produce)	Make, invent or construct an item.
Describe	Give a clear, straightforward description that includes all the main points and links these together logically.
Define	Clearly explain what a particular term means and give an example, if appropriate, to show what you mean.
Explain … how/why	Set out in detail the meaning of something, with reasons. It is often helpful to give an example of what you mean. Start with the topic then give the 'how' or 'why'.
Identify	Distinguish and state the main features or basic facts relating to a topic.
Interpret	Define or explain the meaning of something.
Illustrate	Give examples to show what you mean.
List	Provide the information required in a list rather than in continuous writing.
Outline	Write a clear description that includes all the main points but avoid going into too much detail.
Plan (or devise)	Work out and explain how you would carry out a task or activity.
Select (and present) information	Identify relevant information to support the argument you are making and communicate this in an appropriate way.
State	Write a clear and full account.
Undertake	Carry out a specific activity.
Examples:	
Identify the main features on a digital camera.	
Outline the steps to take to carry out research for an assignment.	

To obtain a merit grade

To obtain a merit you must prove that you can
apply your knowledge in a specific way.

Command words for a merit	Meaning
Analyse	Identify separate factors, say how they relate to each other and how each one relates to the topic.
Classify	Sort your information into appropriate categories before presenting or explaining it.
Compare and contrast	Identify the main factors that apply in two or more situations and explain the similarities and differences or advantages and disadvantages.
Demonstrate	Provide several relevant examples or appropriate evidence which support the arguments you are making. In some vocational areas this may also mean giving a practical performance.
Discuss	Provide a thoughtful and logical argument to support the case you are making.
Explain (in detail)	Provide details and give reasons and/or evidence to clearly support the argument you are making.
Implement	Put into practice or operation. You may also have to interpret or justify the effect or result.
Interpret	Understand and explain an effect or result.
Justify	Give appropriate reasons to support your opinion or views and show how you arrived at these conclusions.
Relate/report	Give a full account, with reasons.
Research	Carry out a full investigation.
Specify	Provide full details and descriptions of selected items or activities.
Examples: Compare and contrast the performance of two different digital cameras. Explain in detail the steps to take to research an assignment.	

To obtain a distinction grade

To obtain a distinction you must prove that you can make a reasoned judgement based on appropriate evidence.

Command words for a distinction	Meaning
Analyse	Identify the key factors, show how they are linked and explain the importance and relevance of each.
Assess	Give careful consideration to all the factors or events that apply and identify which are the most important and relevant, with reasons.
Comprehensively explain	Give a very detailed explanation that covers all the relevant points and give reasons for your views or actions.
Critically comment	Give your view after you have considered all the evidence, particularly the importance of both the relevant positive and negative aspects.
Evaluate	Review the information and then bring it together to form a conclusion. Give evidence to support each of your views or statements.
Evaluate critically	Review the information to decide the degree to which something is true, important or valuable. Then assess possible alternatives, taking into account their strengths and weaknesses if they were applied instead. Then give a precise and detailed account to explain your opinion.
Summarise	Identify/review the main, relevant factors and/or arguments so that these are explained in a clear and concise manner.

Examples:

Assess ten features commonly found on a digital camera.

Analyse your own ability to carry out effective research for an assignment.

TOP TIP

Check that you understand exactly how you need to demonstrate each of the learning outcomes specified in the assignment.

Responding positively

Assignments enable you to demonstrate what you know and how you can apply it. You should respond positively to the challenge and give it your best shot. Being well organised and having confidence in your own abilities helps too, and this is covered in the next section.

Key points

- Read instructions carefully so that you don't make mistakes that can easily be avoided, such as only doing part of the set task.

- Note the assignment deadline on your planner and any interim review dates. Schedule work around these dates to make the most of reviews with your tutor.

- Check your centre's policies relating to assignments, such as how to obtain an extension or query a final grade.

- Expect command words and/or the complexity of a task to be different at higher grades, because you have to demonstrate higher-level skills.

TOP TIP

All your assignments will relate to topics you have covered and work you have done in class. They're not meant to be a test to catch you out.

Action points

1 Check your ability to differentiate between different types of command words by doing this activity.

  a) Prepare a brief description of your usual lifestyle (pass level).

  b) Describe and justify your current lifestyle (merit level).

  c) Critically evaluate your current lifestyle (distinction level).

It would be a good idea to check that your answer is accurate and appropriate by showing it to your tutor at your next tutorial.

TOP TIP

When presenting evidence for an assessment, think about the person who will be looking through it. Plan your 'pitch' well and make it easy for the assessor to match your evidence against the grading criteria.

Sample assignment

Note about assignments

All learners are different and will approach their assignments in different ways.

The sample assignment that follows shows how one learner answered a brief to achieve pass, merit and distinction level criteria. The learner's work shows just one way in which these grading criteria can be evidenced. There are no standard or set answers. If you produce the required evidence for each task then you will achieve the grading criteria covered by the assignment.

Sample assignment front sheet

A completed front sheet must be submitted. This allows your tutor to identify clearly the work you are submitting and to see that it is your own.

Assignments must be submitted by the completion date. Please refer to your centre's submission policy on late work.

Your tutor will be more than happy to give you feedback on your assignment progress to date, before submitting a version for assessment.

This front sheet must be completed by the learner where appropriate and included with the work submitted for assessment.

Learner name	Assessor name
Peter Drake	Mr J Morris

Date issued	Completion date	Submitted on
10 November 2010	10 December 2010	9 December 2010

Qualification	Unit
BTEC Level 3 Diploma in Business	Unit 1: The Business Environment

Assignment title	Two contrasting business organisations

In this assessment you will have opportunities to provide evidence against the following criteria. Indicate the page numbers where the evidence can be found.

Criteria reference	To achieve the criteria the evidence must show that the learner is able to:	Task no.	Page numbers
P1	describe the type of business, purpose and ownership of two contrasting businesses	1	1–2
P2	describe the different stakeholders who influence the purpose of two contrasting businesses	2	2–3
M1	explain the points of view of different stakeholders seeking to influence the aims and objectives of two contrasting organisations	3	3–5
D1	evaluate the influence different stakeholders exert in one organisation	4	5–6

Learner declaration

I certify that the work submitted for this assignment is my own and research sources are fully acknowledged.

Learner signature: Peter Drake   Date: 9 December 2010

This table is very important as it indicates the assessment criterion that is being covered in the particular task.

You must never take someone's words or ideas and use them as if they were your own, unless you indicate clearly in your work where you obtained this information.

The evidence that you provide can take many different forms, such as formal reports, evaluations, notes, verbal recordings, question and answer sessions, logbooks, plans, observations and presentations.

Sample assignment brief

Your assignments will usually begin with a scenario that gives the work a vocational setting.

Always keep focused on the title, as this will help you to keep to the requirements of the assignment tasks.

'Describe' means to provide information that includes relevant features, characteristics, facts, etc.

Unit title	Unit 1: The Business Environment
Qualification	BTEC Level 3 Diploma in Business
Start date	10 November 2010
Deadline date	10 December 2010
Assessor	Mr J Morris

Assignment title	Two contrasting business organisations

The main purpose of this assignment is to:
enable you to describe the different types, purposes and ownership of businesses and to evaluate the influence exerted by stakeholders.

Scenario
You work as a junior researcher for a business magazine and you have been asked to prepare background material for a reporter who is planning a new feature article. The reporter wants to focus on two contrasting business organisations with a presence in your local area, and has asked you for information on them, covering their purpose, ownership and the roles of different stakeholders.

Task 1
You need to select two local organisations for your research. One should be a small organisation. Preferably, one should be in the public sector and the other in the private sector. These two organisations must have a presence in your local area, although this could just be a branch (or shop or office) of a larger organisation.

Describe each business according to its type, purposes and ownership. Does it belong to the public, private or not-for-profit (voluntary) sector? Is it local, national, or international? What about its business activities: does it belong in the primary, secondary or tertiary sector? What are its business purposes, in terms of products and services, and how does the business interact with its customers? Describe the type and structure of the business's ownership, and the implications of this for the way it does business.

This provides evidence for P1

Task 2
Every business has several stakeholders who influence its operations in different ways and to varying degrees. For both your businesses, identify and describe the different stakeholder groups. Consider customers, employees, suppliers, owners, trade unions, employer associations, local and national communities, and governments. You may present the results of your research in the form of a table if this appropriate.

This provides evidence for P2

Task 3
Individual stakeholders (or stakeholder groups) have different points of view about the businesses in which they have an interest and the way they conduct their activities. They will want to influence the aims and objectives of the organisation. Explain the different points of view of the stakeholders in your two organisations.

This provides evidence for M1

Task 4
Now concentrate on just one of your chosen businesses. Carry out an evaluation of the nature and degree of the influence exerted by different stakeholders in that organisation. You will need to use evidence from different sources. You will have to make judgements about the relative importance of different stakeholders in terms of the nature and degree of the influence they exert.

This provides evidence for D1

'Explain' means to provide reasons for a decision, feature, etc.

'Evaluate' means to assess the value, quality or importance of something.

These resources will help you to understand the information and concepts included in the assignment.

Sources of information

Journals
Business Review Magazine (see www.philipallan.co.uk)
The Economist (see www.economist.com)

Websites
Business education website (for learning materials and quizzes) www.bized.ac.uk
BBC Business website www.bbc.co.uk/business
For useful background www.examstutor.com/business (visit the Study Room, see Unit 6)
Official UK statistics www.statistics.gov.uk
Free materials and case studies www.thetimes100.co.uk/home.asp

This brief has been verified as being fit for purpose			
Assessor	Mr J Morris		
Signature	J Morris	Date	11 October 2010
Internal verifier	Ms A Cooke		
Signature	Angela Cooke	Date	11 October 2010

Sample learner work

The introduction describes Tesco plc's business type and purpose, and provides evidence for P1.

Sample learner work: page 1

Two contrasting business organisations

Task 1

How different can two business organisations be?

This research examines two business organisations with a presence in the local area and discusses their very different purposes and ownership. The two businesses are Tesco plc and Ryder's Stores.

Tesco plc

Information extracted from Tesco's website shows that Tesco plc is the largest retailer in the UK and the fourth largest in the world. It is an international business with retail stores in over 20 countries. As a retailer, it belongs to the tertiary sector. Its first purpose is to make a profit for its shareholders. Tesco describes its business purpose as 'to create value for customers to earn their lifetime loyalty', but in the process they need to make a profit for the business and for their shareholders. They believe their success depends on people: 'the people who shop with us and the people who work with us'.

Tesco wants its service to customers to be shaped by two important values, which are given on the company's website (www.tesco.com):
- No one tries harder for their customers.
- Treat people as you like to be treated.

Tesco plc is a retailer and is therefore part of the tertiary sector as it provides a service. It operates internationally, but the UK is where its core business is focused. Globally it has more than 280,000 employees and over 2,100 stores. Around 75 per cent of group sales and profits come from the UK business. Growth in the UK business comes from opening new stores and extensions to existing stores. Sale of non-food items, which is another key part of the company's strategy, also contributes to overall UK growth. Tesco has a well-established and consistent strategy for growth, which has allowed it to strengthen its core UK business and expand into new markets. The reason for the strategy is to broaden the scope of the business so that it can deliver sustainable long-term growth. It has done this by offering the customer new goods and services in expanding UK markets, such as financial services, telecoms and non-food, and by finding new markets abroad, first in Central Europe and Asia, and now also in the United States.

Tesco is a public limited company (plc), which is a business that is owned by its shareholders, run by directors and, most importantly, whose liability is limited. Limited liability means that the investors can only lose the money they have invested and no more. This encourages people to invest in the company. When shares in a plc are first offered for sale to the public, or 'floated', the company is given a 'listing' on the London Stock Exchange. This means it has sold all or part of its business to outside investors. This generates additional funds for the business and can be an important form of fundraising.

Ryder's Stores

Ryder's Stores is a small local business. It is owned by Malcolm Ryder. It is a retailer and like Tesco belongs to the tertiary sector. It provides a service. Malcolm Ryder states that the main purpose is to make a profit for him, the owner. He describes the business purpose as 'providing basic groceries, newspapers, magazines and other goods to the local community'. Malcolm Ryder knows that his success is reliant upon stocking the goods that people want and attracting the local people through having long opening hours and trying to have competitive prices.

There are two employees that work in the store alongside Mr and Mrs Ryder to enable the store to be open between 06.00 and 22.30. There are also six young people who deliver the newspapers and magazines.

The learner has clearly described the type of ownership that exists at Tesco plc, again contributing to P1.

A contrasting description of a small local retailer that is attempting to answer the needs of local shoppers contributes to P1.

The learner has summarised the type of ownership of Ryder's stores, clearly showing how different it is from Tesco plc. P1 has been fully achieved.

Ryder's Store is a sole trader, which means that Malcolm Ryder is the sole owner of the business. He has unlimited liability, which means that he could not only lose the money he has invested in the business but also his private assets such as his house and savings. If he wants additional funds for the business, he has to reinvest profits, use his savings or take out a business loan from his bank.

Task 2

Descriptions of stakeholders for the two businesses

Stakeholders of Tesco plc	Stakeholders of Ryder's Stores
Customers Tesco's customers are the thousands of people who do their shopping in Tesco stores. There are many different types of customer: the loyal ones, who always shop at Tesco stores; occasional customers, who shop at Tesco stores infrequently; adults and young people; male and female; disabled people, ethnic minorities and tourists. There are many ways of describing Tesco's customers, all of whom are stakeholders in its business.	**Customers** Ryder's customers are the people from the local community who shop in the store. There are different types of customer: the loyal ones, who regularly shop at Ryder's; occasional ones, who do not shop frequently at Ryder's; adults and young people; male and female; disabled people; and ethnic minorities. All customers are stakeholders in the business.
Staff Tesco's employees are those who work for the business in return for a salary or wage. There are nearly half a million of these stakeholders worldwide.	**Staff** The two employees and the six young people who deliver the newspapers are stakeholders of Ryder's.
Suppliers These are individuals or businesses who supply goods and services to Tesco. There are large suppliers, such as Cadbury's, and also very small suppliers, such as single farms supplying vegetables.	**Suppliers** These are businesses and individuals who supply goods and services to Ryder's. These include businesses like Hill Top Farm, which supplies free range eggs to the shop, as well as larger suppliers such as Booker Cash and Carry. Malcolm Ryder states that he has a good relationship with his suppliers and that he likes to stay with the same ones so that he can get to know them, they can get to know the types of goods he sells, and then his customers can benefit from the special deals and new products these suppliers offer.
Investors or shareholders These are the individuals and businesses that have invested money into Tesco's and wish to get a decent return on their investment through company dividends.	**The bank** The bank is a stakeholder because it gave Malcolm Ryder a business loan in 2009 to refit the shop.
The Government The UK Government manages Britain's economy and therefore has an interest in how British businesses are performing.	**The Government** The UK Government has an interest in Ryder's because Malcolm is a taxpayer.
Trade unions The unions represent the interests of different workers involved in Tesco's business. They campaign on an ongoing basis for better terms for their members.	**The local community** Ryder's Stores serves the local community. Malcolm Ryder provides bins outside the store to reduce litter. He employs people from the local community. He is also a member of the local Neighbourhood Watch.

This concise summary of the customers, staff and suppliers of the two contrasting businesses contributes evidence for P2.

The learner has provided descriptions of how other stakeholders impact on each of the two businesses, again contributing to P2.

The learner's descriptions of pressure groups and the local community as stakeholders show good understanding of the important role these may play in influencing business activities. P2 has now been fully achieved.

Sample learner work: page 3

Stakeholders of Tesco plc	Stakeholders of Ryder's Stores
Pressure groups A pressure group is an interest group that tries to influence public policy, and especially government legislation, in a particular direction that is consistent with its aims. There are a number of pressure groups that have an interest in Tesco's activities. For example, Friends of the Earth want to make sure that the company is acting in the interests of the environment.	
The local community The local community are important stakeholders. They want to see the local community benefit from the presence of a Tesco store: some want jobs, others are more interested in simply minimising disruption. They will seek to ensure that Tesco's aims and objectives address community issues.	

Task 3

Points of view of Tesco stakeholders

Customers

Tesco's customers exert a strong influence over the aims and objectives of the company's business. If Tesco does not satisfy this group then the business will suffer. They want easy access to store premises and to be able to buy quality products at competitive prices. They are really important because they provide the sales that enable to business to make a profit and be successful. Customers want aims and objectives that are focused on satisfying their needs as customers. Tesco does have a number of objectives associated with customer satisfaction, which customers seek to influence.

Staff

Staff and managers are also stakeholders. They are interested primarily in their job security, prospects and pay. Members of staff want fair pay and working conditions. They will seek to influence the company's aims and objectives to ensure they are well looked after by the business, in terms of good rates of pay, pensions, and the terms and conditions of their employment. Tesco has a number of objectives associated with ensuring the wellbeing of its staff, which includes training targets and promotion opportunities.

Suppliers

Tesco tries to establish and maintain excellent relationships with its suppliers. Suppliers will try and influence the company's aims and objectives to ensure that they obtain regular business, fair treatment and prompt payment. Tesco has set objectives for how suppliers should be treated and also for the quality standards they expect of their suppliers.

Investors

Tesco's investors are primarily interested in dividends and the capital growth of their shares. Shareholders want a good return on their investment and will seek to influence the company's aims and objectives in favour of the payment of dividends. Tesco has been a very profitable company over the last ten years and has paid good dividends to shareholders.

Banks and other financial organisations lending money to Tesco are also stakeholders. Their interests can sometimes come into conflict with those of investors.

These are clear explanations of how customers, staff and suppliers have important points of view that can influence the aims and objectives of Tesco plc. This provides evidence for M1.

A useful summary of the points of view of other important stakeholders also contributes to M1.

A useful summary of the points of view of other important stakeholders also contributes to M1.

The Government

The Government will seek to influence the company's aims and objectives to ensure that Tesco employs as many people as possible, pays its taxes and delivers on environmental issues. Tesco has some of the best policies on ethical and environmental issues, which are helping the Government achieve their targets on these issues. The Government wants employment for the local community too – not just employment of overseas workers.

Trade unions

The unions represent the interests of their members who work for Tesco and will seek to influence the company's aims and objectives in their favour, for example in terms of better pay and conditions.

Pressure groups

These groups are interested in whether the business is acting appropriately in their areas of interest. For example, Greenpeace wants less pollution from Tesco, and will seek to influence the company's aims and objectives in this direction.

The local community

The local community generally want jobs to go to local people and minimum disruption to the local economy and community. They will seek to ensure that Tesco's aims and objectives are addressing community issues.

Points of view of Ryder's Stores stakeholders

Customers

The customers of Ryder's Stores have a strong influence on the business. Without customers there would not be a business. Customers want to be able to access the store at times convenient to them. They also want to be able to buy a range of products and have these products at competitive prices. The customers are the ones who buy the goods and enable the business to make a profit and to be successful.

Staff

Barbara Ryder, the two employees, and the six young people who deliver newspapers are all paid a wage by Malcolm Ryder and as such they are stakeholders. They are all interested in job security and pay rates. They also want good working conditions. Their influence will be to ensure that they get good wage rates and working conditions. The two employees and Mrs Ryder do not have a pension scheme through the business and understand that because they work in a small business they must take out a private pension scheme. Malcolm Ryder has trained his staff himself. One of the employees, Michelle, started as a Young Apprentice and did an NVQ and another course in Retail at the Chamber of Commerce.

Suppliers

The suppliers want to ensure that they maintain Ryder's business and obtain prompt payment for the goods that they supply. They do this by ensuring that Malcolm Ryder knows about their product range and any special deals they have. They set terms and conditions for conducting business with their customers and so have influence on the businesses they supply.

The Bank

The bank is interested in ensuring that they receive regular loan repayments from Malcolm Ryder according to the terms they agreed. Repayments will pay back both the business loan they gave him and the interest on the loan. The bank want Ryder's to be profitable so that they receive their payments.

Malcolm also uses the services of the bank to bank his takings. The bank also seeks to influence Malcolm to maintain his custom.

The Government

The Government will seek to influence all small businesses such as Ryder's Stores to encourage them to employ people, to make profits, so that taxes are paid, and to be ethical and environmentally aware.

The learner shows an understanding of the fact that, even though a business may be small, the points of view of staff, customers and suppliers are still extremely important. This provides evidence for M1.

M1 is fully achieved with a summary of the points of view that the bank and the local community have on the local store.

The learner's descriptions of pressure groups and the local community as stakeholders show good understanding of the important role these may play in influencing business activities. P2 has now been fully achieved.

The learner's evaluation of the different influences that stakeholders have on Tesco plc contributes to D1.

The learner clearly indicates that customers are probably the company's most influential stakeholder group and that Tesco must listen very carefully to what they say. This provides evidence for D1.

Sample learner work: page 5

The local community

The local community are stakeholders. They want Malcolm Ryder to employ local people. They also want him to contribute to minimising disruption and annoyance to the local community. The local community has influenced the business in that Ryder's Stores provides bins to reduce litter and Malcolm Ryder is also a member of the local Neighbourhood Watch. The store is on a parade of shops and Ryder's and Sea Breeze fish and chip shop stay open late. Both shops try to minimise night time noise from their customers because the local community do not want noise disruption. The same applies to Ryder's during their early morning opening hours.

Task 4

Evaluation of the influence different stakeholders exert on Tesco plc

Tesco plc has recently received a lot of criticism over its activities, which is of great interest to a number of its key stakeholders. Tesco is a massive business, which now takes £1 of every £8 spent in UK shops. The company has become increasingly dominant and has expanded into the convenience store and hypermarket sectors of retailing (see www.tescoplc.com/plc/ir/corpgorv/relations/).

Pressure groups such as Friends of the Earth (FOE) point to Tesco's policies of buying up large amounts of land in order to build new stores; its history of fighting battles with local authorities over planning; and how it has brought the company's brand into the high street through its purchase of small convenience stores. The opposition voiced by FOE is summarised in its report 'Calling the shots: How supermarkets get their way in planning decisions'. FOE is a stakeholder that is capable of exerting considerable influence over Tesco's business. Tesco tries to defend itself against such criticisms by repeating that it is always acting in its customers' interests (see Earth Archived Press Releases: www.foe.co.uk/resource/press_releases/tesco_profits_just_not_cri_19092005.html).

Many local governments have expressed concern about the potential impact of major supermarkets on their communities, but they are often unable to do anything about these concerns because the planning system and the strength of the supermarkets are against them.

Tesco also face opposition from smaller pressure groups. A good example is an online group called 'Tescopoly', which is aimed at exposing and limiting what they see as the market-distorting power of the company's business. This campaign group points to cases where Tesco has overstepped its permission to build retail outlets, or where Tesco has admitted to having broken planning regulations (see Tescopoly: How One Shop Came Out on Top and Why It Matters by Andrew Simms).

Tesco also listens very carefully to its shareholders, who along with its customers are probably the company's most influential stakeholders. Tesco appears to be committed to maintaining a good dialogue with its shareholders through organising meetings and presentations, as well as by responding to a wide range of enquiries. They seek shareholder views on a range of issues, from strategy to corporate governance and the environment. In addition to this, the Company Secretary's office, Investor Relations and other teams within the business interact with shareholders on a regular basis – most regularly with their institutional shareholders (see www.tescoplc.com/plc/ir/corpgorv/relations/).

Tesco's customers are probably their most important stakeholders and exert the strongest influence. Different types of customers have different needs, some customers working all day and wanting to shop at night and vice versa; consequently, Tesco has a major store, 'Tesco Extra', open 24 hours, all day and night. There are other formats that have been developed to meet customer needs, such as Tesco Online and Tesco Express. All these developments, says Tesco, are the result of research among their customers. The company appears to respond to this stakeholder group's interests very well. Without this group of stakeholders, Tesco wouldn't have a business, so they respond very quickly to customers concerns about pricing, product range and

This review of how an important stakeholder is exerting considerable influence on Tesco's activities and how Tesco combats these criticisms contributes to D1.

Another summary of how this smaller pressure group is exerting influence and forcing Tesco to respond, again contributes to D1.

This shows the important influence exerted by those who own the company and how Tesco reacts to such influence, providing evidence for D1.

This review of how Tesco is responding to stakeholder influence indicates good research around the topic. This contributes to the achievement of D1.

Sample learner work: page 6

quality (see *Scoring Points: How Tesco is Winning Customer Loyalty* by Terry Hunt, Clive Humby and Tim Phillips).

Tesco has taken a number of initiatives as a result of customer influence recently. It has reduced the amount of in-store waste going to landfill by one-third in the space of a year. It has supported local community campaigns. It has also begun educating consumers on the carbon footprints of what they buy. Tesco has set rigorous objectives on reducing its carbon footprint. The company intends to lead the way on this issue by dramatically reducing its own carbon footprint and making low-carbon products accessible and affordable for consumers (see www.tescoplc.com/plc/ir/corpgorv/relations/).

The British Government wholeheartedly supports Tesco in this strategy. The long-running 'Computers for Schools' programme has been very successful. New initiatives on food content and labelling; promoting exercise, balanced lifestyles and healthy eating; and extending efforts to reduce negative environmental impacts and maximise positive ones are further examples of their responses to stakeholder influence.

Some MPs have criticised Tesco for promoting binge drinking by heavily discounting alcohol in their stores. Tesco have since responded to this by agreeing to work with the Government to make people more aware of the dangers of excessive drinking. The company is clearly influenced by Parliament and the Government on a number of issues (see the article by Joe Sinclair in the Independent, Thursday, 21 February 2008).

Tesco has recently been working with the Government to help those without jobs. The venture with Tesco is part of the Department for Work and Pensions' 'Pathways to Work' programme, which has already found work for some 4,000 people on incapacity benefit. The programme is among the Government's reform initiatives aimed at ensuring that people who receive benefits do not do so doing nothing in return. The scheme allows willing people to be put to work at Tesco for a week to prepare them for a job. This will be followed by training and support to help them compete in the job market. Tesco will take some of them on in permanent jobs; others will go on to employment elsewhere. This is a good example of Tesco responding to the Government's influence of wanting a British successful business to be seen to be helping those in need (see www. personneltoday.com – 'In-training Employability celebrates launch of Pathways to Work', 15th August 2008).

The influence of the Government on Tesco is massive in terms of environmental and ethical issues. Tesco is committed to the principles of 'reduce, re-use, recycle' in tackling waste and too much packaging in their operations and for customers. They have targets to minimise the amount of waste sent to landfill, to reduce the amount of packaging on their products and to give out fewer carrier bags. They are also involved in initiatives and trials to deal with other important issues, such as helping customers to recycle more and to reduce food waste in their operations and by customers (see www.tescoplc.com/plc/ir/corpgorv/relations/).

How the company sources its products can have a significant environmental impact. Tesco has policies in place to ensure that key supplies are sourced responsibly. They aim to work with suppliers and others to ensure that their policies are sound and rigorously implemented. Where appropriate, they play an active role in cross-industry groups that have the power to deliver wider change, which is necessary for them to deliver their commitments (see www.tescoplc.com/plc/ir/corpgorv/relations/).

In conclusion, it appears that different stakeholders have conflicting interests and views. Supermarket suppliers want higher profit margins, faster payment and more warning of changes in purchasing. Consumers want lower prices, a wider range of products and easy access. Employees want better terms and conditions of employment, whereas shareholders want costs kept to a minimum to increase profits. There are various activities that show that Tesco responds well to certain stakeholder influences and there are other areas, such as the huge reduction in small independent retail businesses due to the company's growth, and the low prices paid for meat to some farmers, where perhaps they do not respond so well. It is a balancing act for them in making sure that no particular stakeholder is upset too much by the company's decisions. In my opinion, it is understandable that Tesco responds quickly to important stakeholders, such as customers, shareholders, some pressure groups and the Government, but is less responsive to the business community and its employees.

The learner has also discussed the important influence exerted by suppliers, again contributing to D1.

The conclusion to the learner's evaluation of the influence of different stakeholders on Tesco plc provides further evidence and D1 is now fully achieved.

The learner has correctly identified the significant influence exerted by the UK Government and has raised relevant points, effectively contributing to D1.

At this level it is very important that you clearly reference where you have obtained information for your assignment.

Sample learner work: page 7

Bibliography

Websites

Earth Archived Press releases:
www.foe.co.uk/resource/press_releases/tesco_profits_just_not_cri_19092005.html

www.personneltoday.com ('In-training Employability celebrates launch of Pathways to Work', 15 August 2008)

Tesco relations with stakeholders: www.tescoplc.com/plc/ir/corpgov/relations/

Other publications

Hunt, Dooley, Dransfield, Goymer, Guy and Richards – *BTEC National Business: Book 1: Student Book 1 (BTEC Nationals)* (Pearson, 2006)

Hunt T, Humby, C and Phillips, T – *Scoring Points: How Tesco is Winning Customer Loyalty* (2008)

Simms, A – *Tescopoly: How One Shop Came Out on Top and Why It Matters* (2008)

Sample assessor's comments

> Here you have the chance to say whether you agree with the feedback given by the assessor. This is an important part of the assessment process.

> This column indicates whether you have met the performance criteria. 'Y' means you have, 'N' means that you have not.

Qualification	BTEC Level 3 Diploma in Business	Year	2010–2011
Unit number and title	Unit 1: The Business Environment	Learner name	Peter Drake

Grading criteria	Achieved?
P1 describe the type of business, purpose and ownership of two contrasting businesses	Y
P2 describe the different stakeholders who influence the purpose of two contrasting businesses	Y
M1 explain the points of view of different stakeholders seeking to influence the aims and objectives of two contrasting organisations	Y
D1 evaluate the influence different stakeholders exert in one organisation	Y

Learner feedback

I found this assignment quite difficult. Tesco and Ryder's Stores are so different. There seemed to be so much to say about Tesco. Because Ryder's is a smaller business I got to meet and talk to the owner and found it easier to understand, but there didn't seem to be as much to write.

Assessor feedback

For Task 1, you have successfully described the type of business, purpose and ownership of two contrasting businesses. You selected Tesco plc as a large multi-national, profit-making organisation and Ryder's Stores as a small, local business. You have explained who the stakeholders are for each organisation. You have clearly explained the points of view of the different stakeholders for Tesco and Ryder's Stores. For D1, you have successfully discussed Tesco's relationship with its stakeholders and the extent of influence that some have compared to others. You have made good use of examples in D1 to explain your points. You have therefore been awarded P1, P2, M1 and D1. Well done, a very good assignment.

You have covered the set tasks fully and achieved all the criteria for this unit in this assignment at pass, merit and distinction level. What you have learned from this project will give you a tremendous advantage in your assignments for the units to come.

Action plan

Continue to read widely around the subject matter and keep abreast of how both organisations will continue to respond to stakeholder influences in the future.

Assessor signature	J Morris	Date	19 January 2011
Learner signature	Peter Drake	Date	20 January 2011

> The action planning process is essential as this plan clearly indicates what you need to do to improve your work in the future.

Activity

If you were doing this assignment, which businesses would you use?

List four reasons why

1

2

3

4

Step Seven: Work productively as a member of a group

Case study: Working as a team

Lee is a learner on the BTEC National Diploma in Business and has a part-time weekend job at a local distribution warehouse. The manager asks Lee and five other members of staff to form a team. He asks the team to come up with recommendations for how one part of the warehouse could be reorganised to make it easier to assemble goods for distribution.

The manager selects the six members based on their individual skills. The team meet for the first time and introduce themselves. Lee is creative, Carla has good leadership skills, Leroy is very practical and good at getting things done, Zoe is good at planning and anticipating problems, Bruno is skilled at design, and Paul is hardworking and always sees things through to the end. Carla is asked by the manager to be the team leader.

During their meetings, Carla always listens to the opinions of other members of the team. She praises and encourages team members when they produce good work. She discusses ideas and criticises constructively.

In the warehouse area under consideration, currently products are positioned in alphabetical order. When picking an order,

assemblers simply start at the 'A's and work their way down the alphabet.

The project team notice that some products are ordered far more frequently than others. Therefore, they recommend that the layout is changed so that the fastest-selling lines are positioned at the beginning of the flow, with the slower lines at the end. As a result of this reorganisation, the average time taken for order assemblers to put together an order is reduced, which significantly increases productivity. The manager is delighted with the team's work and plans more project work based on the work of effective teams.

Reflection points

Why do you think it is important for a team to have a clear goal before they start work?

Why is it important for team members to possess different skills?

If Carla was not a good communicator and did not allow anyone to express their point of view, how do you think this would this affect the overall success of the team?

In your private life, you can choose your own friends, whereas at work you are paid to work alongside many people; whether you like them or not.

This applies at school or college too. Hopefully, by now, you've outgrown wanting to only work with your best friends on every project.

You may not be keen on everyone in your team, but you should still be pleasant and co-operative. This may be harder if you are working with a partner than in a large group.

Sometimes you may be the group leader. This may inspire you, or fill you with dread. You won't be expected to develop team-leader skills overnight, but it helps if you know the basics.

First, you should understand how groups and teams work and why good teamwork is considered vital by employers.

Working in groups and teams

If you have a full- or part-time job, you already belong to a working group, or team. At school or college your class is an example of a working group.

All working groups have some common characteristics:

- doing the same type of work – though in the workplace you probably have different roles or responsibilities
- a group leader or supervisor
- a reason for working together, such as studying for the same qualification or tackling an area of work too large for someone to do it alone
- group members are dependent on each other in some way; at work you may have to cover someone's workload if they are absent
- group members concentrate on their individual achievements and success.

A team is different. As a team member you have a specific objective to achieve **together** – and this is more important than the goals of individual team members.

> **TOP TIP**
>
> Understanding how groups and teams function will help you be a better team worker and a better team leader.

These are the characteristics of a team.

- Team members have a team goal which is more important than any personal goals.
- Team members have complementary skills so that the team can achieve more than individuals working alone could achieve.
- Work is allocated to play to each person's strengths and talents.
- The team members give each other encouragement and support.
- There is collective responsibility for achieving the goal.

A good team leader acts as facilitator and motivator, and gives practical support and guidance.

Working in a team has many benefits. Team members can learn from each other and combine their skills to do a better job more quickly. Working with other people is often more enjoyable than working alone, too. Many industries rely a lot on efficient group working, from IT teams to health workers and the emergency services.

> **TOP TIP**
>
> Focusing on the task rather than on personalities is the first step in learning to work with different people, whose views may not match your own.

There are many benefits to be gained from working as a team.

Being a good team member

Everyone wants team members who are talented, positive, cheerful and full of energy. These are the key areas to focus on if you wish to be a good team member.

- **Your social skills.** This includes being courteous, treating other people as you wish to be treated, saying 'please' when you want something and thanking people who do you a favour.

- **Your temperament**. Expect people to have different views and opinions from you and don't take offence if someone disagrees with you. If you lose your temper easily, learn to walk away before you say something you may regret.

- **Your communication skills.** This includes talking and listening!
  Practise saying what you mean clearly, accurately and succinctly. Be prepared to give good reasons to justify your arguments and ideas.
  Allow people to finish what they're saying, without interruption, before you talk. Never shout people down. Think before you speak so that you don't upset people with tactless remarks. If you inadvertently do so, apologise.

- **Your commitment.** Always keep your promises and never let anyone down when they are depending upon you. Always do your fair share of the work, even if you don't agree with all the decisions made by your team. Tell people promptly if you are having problems so there is time to solve them. Be loyal to your team when you're talking to other people.

Being the team leader

It can be difficult to strike a balance between 'leading' the team and working with friends. You need to inspire and motivate your team without being bossy or critical.

Important points to remember about being a team leader

- Lead by example. Stay pleasant, consistent and control your temper, even under pressure.

- Everyone is different. Your ways of working may not always be the best.

- Be prepared to listen and contribute positively to a discussion.

- Encourage quieter team members to join in discussions by asking for their views.

- Be prepared to do whatever you ask other people to do.

- Note down what you say you will do, so that you don't forget.

- Discuss alternatives with people rather than giving orders.

- Be sensitive to other people's feelings. They may have personal problems or issues that affect their behaviour.

- Learn the art of persuasion.

- Act as peacemaker. Help people reach a compromise when necessary.

- Give team members the credit for their hard work or good ideas.

- Admit your mistakes. Look for a positive solution and think about what can be learned for the future, rather than making excuses.

- Praise and encourage team members who are working hard.

- Make criticisms constructively, and in private.

- Be assertive (put forward your point of view firmly) rather than aggressive (attacking other people to defend yourself).

Some notes of caution about being a team leader

- Try to look pleasant and don't glare at people who interrupt you unexpectedly.

- Never talk about team members behind their backs.

- Don't gossip, exaggerate to make a point, spread rumours, speculate or tell lies.

- Don't expect to get your own way all the time – all good leaders back down on occasion.

- Never criticise any colleagues in front of other people. Speak to them in private and keep it constructive.

TOP TIP

Excellent ideas often come from quiet team members. Encourage everyone to make suggestions so that you don't overlook any valuable contributions.

Key points

- There are many benefits of working in a group or as a team. These include mutual support, companionship and the exchange of ideas.
- You will be expected to work co-operatively with other people at work, and during many course assignments.

- It isn't easy learning to be a team leader. Team leaders should be fair, consistent and pleasant to work with, as well as loyal and sensitive to the needs of team members.

Action points

1 Identify the role of teamwork in your area of study. Identify the team's goal and any factors you think will contribute towards its success.

2 Decide how you would handle each of the following difficult situations if you were the team leader. If you can, discuss your ideas with a friend in your class.

   a) The team needs to borrow a college video camera to record an event being held tonight. Your tutor tells you that the one you reserved last week is not working and the rest are out on loan.

   b) A member of your team has personal problems so you have given him less work to do. Now you've been accused of having favourites.

   c) A team member is constantly letting everyone down because of poor work and non-attendance at group meetings.

   d) Two team members have disagreed about how to do a task. You're not bothered how they do it as long as it gets done properly, and by the deadline.

   e) A team member becomes very aggressive whenever she is challenged in any way – no matter how mildly.

3 Identify someone who has inspired you because they've been an excellent leader. This could be someone you've met, a fictional character or a famous person. Note down what it is about them that impressed you.

TOP TIP

Team working, and bouncing ideas around, produces quicker and better results than working in isolation.Businesses actively encourage team working.

Activity: Teamwork

1 The following are examples of situations you may face when working as part of a team (or when leading a team). Indicate whether the following statements are 'True' or 'False':

a) An effective team usually has a team leader. 　　　　　　　　　　**True**　　**False**

b) Every team member has different objectives. 　　　　　　　　　　**True**　　**False**

c) The team objective is more important than any personal goals. 　**True**　　**False**

d) Team members should never give each other help and support. 　**True**　　**False**

e) Most people enjoy working as part of a team. 　　　　　　　　　**True**　　**False**

f) Team members will have different views and opinions. 　　　　　**True**　　**False**

Teamworking is a complex process and success depends on factors including:

- how the team is formed and how members bond
- how the team is led
- the complementary skill sets of team members
- how skills are developed within the team.

2 It is often said that the work output of an effective team is usually greater than the sum of the individual contributions. What do you think this statement means?

3 You have been appointed team leader for a group of learners that has the task of surveying local businesses to identify different types of ownership. As team leader, what are the key factors that you need to consider to make sure your team works effectively to achieve its goal?

4 Think of your favourite sports team, or any other familiar team. Explain why your chosen team is effective or ineffective.

Step Eight: Understand how to research and analyse information

Case study: Toby's research

Toby is the marketing research manager for a publisher that produces a monthly magazine called *Fit for Life*. This magazine is aimed at young men and contains articles and information about how young males can pursue a healthy lifestyle.

Toby wants to analyse the marketplace to see if there is an opportunity to publish a new magazine aimed at middle-aged men, between the ages of 35 and 65. He already has some information to help him in his analysis: other members of the marketing team have told him

their opinions about this opportunity; he has a number of market research reports on the middle-aged fitness and health market which he produced two months ago; information in the form of bar charts and line graphs on market trends; and a number of relevant websites where information about the marketplace can be found. He also has access to a detailed report carried out by researchers at a local university on the state of the middle-aged male health and fitness market.

Using the case study above, answer the following questions about Toby's research:

1 When is Toby using:

a) verbal information

b) printed information

c) graphical information

d) electronic information

2 Primary research is original data prepared by you, whereas secondary research is information prepared by someone else. When is Toby using primary research?

3 When is Toby using secondary research?

4 Why do you think it is important to have relevant up-to-date information when making important decisions?

As a BTEC Level 3 National learner, you often have to find information for yourself. This skill will be invaluable in your working life, and if you continue your studies at higher education (HE) level. Sometimes the information will give you a better understanding of a topic, at other times you will research to obtain information for a project or assignment. Sometimes you may be so interested in something that you want to find out more without being told to do so!

Whatever your reason, and no matter where your information can be found, there is a good and not so good way to go about the task. This section will help if you can't find what you want, or find too much, or drift aimlessly around a library, or watch a demonstration and don't know what to ask afterwards.

Types of information

There are many types of information and many different sources. Depending on the task, these are the sources you may need to consult.

- **Verbal information.** This includes talking to friends, colleagues at work, members of your family, listening to experts explain what they do, interviewing people, talking to sales reps at an exhibition or customers about a product.

- **Printed information.** This includes information printed in newspapers, journals, magazines, books, posters, workshop manuals, leaflets and catalogues. The type of magazine or newspaper you read may have its own slant on the information, which you may have to take into account (see page 69).

- **Written information.** This includes course notes and handouts, reports and other documents in the workplace. If you want to use written information from work, you must check this is allowed, and that it doesn't contain confidential material such as financial information or staff names and addresses.

- **Graphical information.** This includes illustrations, pictures, cartoons, line drawings, graphs and photographs. Graphics can make something clearer than words alone. For example, a satnav instruction book might contain illustrations to show different procedures.

- **Electronic information.** This includes information from electronic sources such as DVDs, CD-ROMs, searchable databases, websites, podcasts, webinars (**seminars** online), emails and text messages. The huge amount of information available online is both a help and a hindrance. You can find information quickly, but the source may be unreliable, out-of-date, inaccurate or inappropriate (see page 62.)

TOP TIP

Too much information is as bad as too little, because it's overwhelming. The trick is to find good quality, relevant information and know when to call a halt to your search.

Finding what you need

Spend a few minutes planning what to do before you start looking for information. This can save a lot of time later on.

The following steps will help you to do this.

1 Make sure you understand exactly what it is you need to know so that you don't waste time looking for the wrong thing.

2 Clarify your objectives to narrow down your search. Think about why the information is wanted and how much detail you need. For example, learners studying BTEC Nationals in Engineering and Performing Arts may both be researching 'noise' for their projects but they are likely to need different types of information and use it in different ways.

3 Identify your sources and check you know how to use them. You need to choose sources that are most likely to provide information relevant to your objectives. For example, an Engineering learner might find information on noise emissions in industry journals and by checking out specialist websites.

4 Plan and schedule your research. Theoretically, you could research information forever. Knowing when to call a halt takes skill. Write a schedule that states when you must stop looking and start sorting the information.

5 Store your information safely in a labelled folder. This folder should include printouts or photocopies of articles, notes about events you have attended or observed, photographs you've taken or sketches you've drawn. Divide your information under topic headings to make it easier to find. When you're ready to start work, re-read your assignment brief and select the items that are most closely related to the task you are doing.

TOP TIP

Allocate time for research as part of your assignment task. Take into account any interim deadlines as well as the final deadline for completing the work.

Primary and secondary research, and the law of copyright

There are two ways to research information. One is known as primary research, the other is secondary research.

Primary research

Primary research involves finding new information about an issue or topic. This might include finding out people's views about a product or interviewing an expert. When carrying out interviews, you will need to design a survey or questionnaire. Your primary research might also include observing or experiencing something for yourself, and recording your feelings and observations.

Secondary research

Secondary research involves accessing information that already exists in books, files, newspapers or on CD-ROMs, computer databases or the internet, and assessing it against your objectives.

This information has been prepared by other people and is available to anyone. You can quote from an original work provided you acknowledge

the source of your information. You should put this acknowledgement in your text or in the bibliography to your text; do not claim it as your own research. You must include the author's name, year of publication, the title and publisher, or the web address if it is an online article. You should practise listing the sources of articles so that you feel confident writing a bibliography. Use the guidance sheet issued by your centre to help you. This will illustrate the style your centre recommends. (See also page 65.)

The trick with research is to choose the best technique to achieve your objectives and this may mean using a mix of methods and resources. For example, if you have to comment on an industry event you might go to it, make notes, interview people attending, observe the event (perhaps take a video camera), and read any newspaper reports or online comments.

TOP TIP

Always make sure you make a note of where you get information from (your source). Keep it safely as it can be very difficult later on to work out where it came from!

People as a source of information

If you want to get the most out of interviewing someone, or several people, you need to prepare carefully in advance.

The following points give some general advice about getting the most out of face-to-face interviews.

- Make sure you know what questions to ask to get the information you need.
- Explain why you want the information.
- Don't expect to be told confidential or sensitive information.
- Write clear notes so that you remember who told you what, and when. (See also page 64.)

- Note the contact details of the person you are interviewing and ask whether they mind if you contact them again should you think of anything later or need to clarify your notes.
- Thank them for their help.

If you want to ask a lot of people for their opinion you may want to conduct a survey. You will need to design a questionnaire and analyse the results. This will be easier if you ask for **quantitative** responses – for example yes/no, true/false or ratings on a five-point scale – rather than opinions.

- Give careful thought to your representative sample (people whose opinions are relevant to the topic).

- Decide how many people to survey so that the results mean something.
- Keep the survey relatively short.
- Thank people who complete it.
- Analyse the results, and write up your conclusions promptly.

TOP TIP

Test your questionnaire on volunteers before you 'go live' to check that there are no mistakes and the questions are easy to understand. Make any amendments before you conduct your 'real' survey.

Asking someone who knows a lot about a topic can be informative.

Avoiding pitfalls

Wikipedia is a good online source that covers many topics, and often in some depth. It is popular and free. However, it has an open-content policy, which means that anyone can contribute to and edit entries. People may post information, whether it is correct or not. Wikipedia is moving towards greater checks on entries, but it is still sensible to check out information you find on this site somewhere else.

Apart from inaccuracy, you may find other problems with information you obtain through research, especially material found online.

- **Out-of-date material.** Check the date of everything and keep only the latest version of books, newspapers or magazines. Yesterday's news may be of little use if you are researching something topical.
- **Irrelevant details.** Often, only part of an article will be relevant to your search. For example, if you are forecasting future trends in an area of work, you do not need information about its history or related problems. When learners are struggling, they sometimes 'pad out' answers with irrelevant information. If you've researched properly you can avoid this by having enough

relevant information for your purposes.

- **Invalid assumptions.** This means someone has jumped to the wrong conclusion and made 2 + 2 = 5. You might do this if you see two friends chatting and think they are talking about you – whether they are or not! You can avoid problems in this area by double-checking your ideas and getting evidence to support them.

- **Bias.** This is when people hold strong views about a topic, or let their emotions or prejudices affect their judgement. An obvious example is asking a keen football fan for an objective evaluation of their team's performance!

- **Vested interests.** People may argue in a certain way because it's in their own interests to do so. For example, when the Government said Home Information Packs must be prepared for all properties being sold, the Association of Home Information Pack Providers was in favour because it trains the people who prepare the packs. The National Association of Estate Agents and Royal Institution of Chartered Surveyors were not because they thought they would lose business if people were put off selling their houses.

> **TOP TIP**
>
> Don't discard information that is affected by bias or vested interests. Just make it clear you know about the problem and have taken it into account.

Reading for a purpose

You may enjoy reading or you may find it tedious or difficult. If so, it helps to know that there are different ways to read, depending on what you're doing. For example, you wouldn't look for a programme in a TV guide in the same way that you would check an assignment for mistakes. You can save time and find information more easily if you use the best method of reading to suit your purpose. The following are some examples of ways of reading.

- **Skim reading** is used to check new information and get a general overview.

To skim a book chapter read the first and last paragraphs, the headings, subheadings and illustrations. It also helps to read the first sentence of each paragraph.

> **TOP TIP**
>
> News articles are written with the key points at the beginning, so concentrate on the first paragraph or two. Feature articles have a general introduction and important information is contained in the main text.

- **Scanning** is used to see whether an article contains something you need – such as key words, dates or technical terms. Focus on capital or initial letters for a name, and figures for a date. Technical terms may be in bold or italics.

- **Light reading** is usually done for pleasure when you are relaxed, for example, reading a magazine article. You may not remember many facts afterwards, so this sort of reading isn't suitable for learning something or assessing its value.

- **Word-by-word reading (proofreading)** is important so that you don't miss anything, such as the dosage instructions for a strong medicine. You should proofread assignments before you submit them.

- **Reading for study (active reading)** means being actively involved so that you understand the information. It is rare to be naturally good at this, so you might have to work to develop this skill.

Developing critical and analytical skills

Developing critical and analytical skills involves looking at information for any flaws in the arguments. These skills are important when you progress to work or higher education (HE), so it's useful to practise them now on your BTEC Level 3 National course.

A useful technique for understanding, analysing, evaluating and remembering what you are reading is **SQ4R**.

SQ4R is an effective method. It consists of six steps.

1 Survey first, to get a general impression. Scan the information to see what it is about, when it was written and by whom. The source, and the reason it was written, may be important. Most newspapers, for example, have their own 'slant' that affects how information is presented.

2 Question your aims for reading this material. What are you hoping to find? What questions are you expecting it to answer?

3 Read the information three or four times. The first time, aim to get a general idea of the content. Use a dictionary to look up any new words. Then read more carefully to really understand what the writer means.

4 Respond by thinking critically about the information and how it relates to the topic you are studying. Does it answer your queries partially, fully or not at all? What information is factual and what is based on opinion? Is there evidence to support these opinions? Is there a reason why the author has taken this standpoint? Do you agree with it? How does it link to other information you have read? What is the opposite argument and is there any evidence to support this? Overall, how useful is this information?

5 Record the information by noting the key points. Use this to refresh your memory, if necessary, rather than re-reading the article.

6 Review your notes against the original to check you have included all important points. If you are also preparing a presentation, reviewing your notes will help you to remember key points more easily.

TOP TIP

SQ4R is just one method of reading for study. Research others and adapt them to suit your own style.

Taking good notes

There are many occasions when you need to take notes, such as when a visiting speaker is talking to your class. There's no point taking notes unless you write them in a way that will allow you to use them later.

Note-taking is a personal activity. Some people prefer to make diagrammatical sketches with key points in boxes linked by arrows; others prefer to write a series of bullet points. You will develop your own style, but the following hints and tips might help you at the start.

- Use A4 lined paper, rather than a notebook, so that you have more space and don't need to turn over so often.
- When you're reading for study, make sure you have a dictionary, pen, notepad and highlighter to hand.
- Leave a wide margin to record your own comments or queries.
- Put a heading at the top, such as the speaker's name and topic, as well as the date.
- If you are making notes from a book or an article, remember SQ4R and read it several times first. Your notes will only be effective if you understand the information.
- Don't write in complete sentences – it takes too long.
- Leave spaces for later additions or corrections.
- Use headings to keep your notes clear and well organised.
- Only write down relevant information, including key words and phrases.

- Highlight, underline or use capitals for essential points.
- Never copy chunks of text – always use your own words.
- Clearly identify quotations, and record your sources, so that you can cite them in your work. (Note the author's name, title, publisher, date and place of publication and the page number.)

TOP TIP

Make sure your information is accurate, up-to-date, relevant and valid. Be aware of bias, and don't confuse fact with opinion.

Key points

- Useful information may be verbal, printed, written, graphical or electronic.
- Effective research means knowing exactly what you are trying to find and where to look. Know how reference media are stored in your library and how to search online. Store important information carefully.
- Primary research is original data you obtain yourself. Secondary research is information prepared by someone else. If you use this, you must quote your sources in a bibliography.
- You can search for information by skimming and scanning, and read in different ways. Reading for study means actively involving yourself with the text, questioning what you are reading and making notes to help your own understanding.
- Read widely around a topic to get different viewpoints. Don't accept everything you read as correct. Think about how it fits with other information you have obtained.
- Taking notes is a personal skill that takes time to develop. Start by using A4 lined pages with a margin, set out your notes clearly and label them. Only record essential information.

Action points

- Working with a friend, look back at the sources of information listed on page 60. For each type, identify examples of information relevant to your course that you could obtain from each source. See how many you can list under each type.
- Check your ability to find the information you need by answering each of the questions in **Activity: Finding information** on the next page. For any questions you get wrong, your first research task is to find out the correct answers as quickly as you can.
- To check your ability to skim and scan information, improve your ability to differentiate fact from opinion, summarise text and much more, go to page 92 for information on how to access useful websites.
- Check your ability to sort fact from opinion and spot vested interests by completing **Activity: Let's give you a tip...** on page 68. Check your ideas with the answers on page 91.

TOP TIP

Make a note of any information that you are struggling to understand so that you can discuss it with your tutor.

Activity: Finding information

Answer the following questions about finding information.

a) Four types of information that are available from the library in your centre, besides books, are:

1

2

3

4

b) When I visit the library, the way to check if a book I want is available is:

c) The difference between borrowing a book on short-term loan and on long-term loan is:

Short-term loan:

Long-term loan:

d) The journals that are stocked by the library that are relevant to my course include:

e) Useful information on the intranet at my centre includes:

f) Searchable databases and online magazines I can access include:

g) The quickest way to check if a book or journal contains the type of information I need is to:

h) The difference between a search engine, a portal, a directory site and a forum is:

i) Bookmarking useful websites means:

j) In addition to suggesting websites, Google can also provide the following types of information:

k) Specialist websites which provide useful information related to my course include:

l) Useful tips I would give to people starting on my course who need to find out information are:

Activity: Let's give you a tip...

In 2009, many businesses were struggling thanks to the credit crunch and falling consumer demand. Some, like Woolworths, closed down altogether. Others laid off staff, or announced wage cuts. Despite this, the Government approved recommendations by the Low Pay Commission to increase the minimum wage rate from October. Although the rise was only small, many unions, including Unison and Usdaw, agreed it was better than a freeze, which had been wanted by the British Chambers of Commerce and the British Retail Consortium.

The Government also announced new laws to stop restaurants and bars using tips to top up staff pay to the minimum level. *The Independent* newspaper claimed its 'fair tips, fair pay' campaign had won the day. It also reported that the British Hospitality Association was claiming this could result in up to 45,000 job losses. The Unite union also carried out a campaign and its General Secretary claimed the decision a triumph for the poorly paid. Not everyone agreed. Some thought there should be no tipping at all, as in Australia. Others said the Canadian system was best – wages are low but generous tips are left, and this motivates staff to give excellent service.

a) Look at the table below. In your view, which of the statements are facts and which are opinions? In each case, justify your view.

Statement	Fact or opinion?	Justification
i) Having a national minimum wage helps low-paid workers.		
ii) Over one million people will benefit from the minimum wage increase.		
iii) The new law on tips will stop restaurants paying below minimum wage rates.		
iv) Using the Australian system of no tips would be better.		
v) The Canadian system guarantees good service.		
vi) 45,000 job losses will occur in the hospitality industry.		

b) All newspapers have their own way of putting forward the news. Go to page 92 to see how you can access a website which will help you to compare the way that news is reported in different newspapers.

Compare six different newspapers and make notes on:
i) the type of stories covered

ii) the way views are put forward.

Activity: Conducting research

You will need to carry out research on Tesco plc, the retail business. Go to your learning resource centre and find an example of printed information on the size, financial position and marketplace of Tesco plc. This information may be found in business journals, newspapers or in textbooks.

Explain what the information is saying.

Now try to find some graphical information, either about the marketplace of Tesco plc or its current financial situation, and explain what the graph is showing.

Go to the Tesco plc website and obtain general electronic information about Tesco plc.

Explain briefly what the electronic information is saying.

You should now have three separate pieces of information about Tesco plc. Is this primary or secondary research?

If you had designed a questionnaire and surveyed customers at your local Tesco store, would this be primary or secondary research?

You have arranged to meet the manager of the local Tesco store and you are going to ask them about the way the business is organised. What advance preparations would you make?

Step Nine: Make an effective presentation

Case study: Teresa's presentation

Teresa is a trainee human resource manager at her local council. She was recruited to this position having obtained her BTEC National Diploma in Business and then a degree in Human Resource Management. She has to give a presentation to the council chamber on the future employment needs of the organisation. She has two weeks to prepare. She tries to remember what she was taught on her previous courses about giving presentations. She decides that she will use PowerPoint with supporting handouts, and begins researching relevant information on future employment needs.

Having obtained this information, she begins to produce her PowerPoint presentation and handouts. She rehearses the presentation to ensure her timing is correct and tries to anticipate questions that she might be asked. The day before the presentation, Teresa visits the venue to make sure that everything she needs is in place.

Reflection points

Teresa has spent a great deal of time preparing for the presentation. Why do you think it is important to plan very carefully and to rehearse before giving a presentation?

If Teresa had been asked to give a group presentation with a number of other members of the human resource team, what other factors would have to be taken into consideration when planning the presentation?

Making a presentation can be nerve-wracking. It involves several skills, including planning, preparation and communication. It tests your ability to work in a team, speak in public and use IT (normally PowerPoint.) You also have to stay calm under pressure. However, as it is excellent practice for your future, you can expect presentations to be a common method of assessing your performance.

TOP TIP

When you're giving a presentation, keep to time, get to the point and use your time well.

Good planning and preparation

Being well prepared, and rehearsing beforehand, helps your confidence and your presentation. The following points will help you to do this.

- If you're part of a team, find out everyone's strengths and weaknesses and divide work fairly taking these into account. Decide how long each person should speak, who should introduce the team and who will summarise at the end.

- Take into account your time-scale, resources and team skills. A simple, clear presentation is better – and safer – than a complicated one.

- If you're using PowerPoint, make slides more interesting by avoiding a series of bulleted lists and including artwork. Print PowerPoint notes for the audience. Use a fuller set of notes for yourself, as a prompt.

- Check the venue and time.

- Decide what to wear and check it's clean and presentable.
- Prepare, check and print your handouts.
- Decide, as a team, the order in which people will speak, bearing in mind the topic.
- Discuss possible questions and how to answer them.
- Rehearse beforehand to check your timings.

If you prepare properly you can really enjoy giving a presentation.

On the day, you can achieve a better performance if you:

- arrive in plenty of time
- calm your nerves by taking deep breaths before going in front of your audience
- introduce yourself clearly, and smile at the audience
- avoid reading from your screen or your notes
- explain what you are going to do – especially if giving a demonstration – do it and then review what you've done
- say you will deal with questions at the end of any demonstration
- answer questions honestly – don't exaggerate, guess or waffle
- respond positively to all feedback, which should be used to improve your performance next time.

Key points

- When making a presentation, prepare well, don't be too ambitious and have several rehearsals.
- When giving a demonstration, explain first what you are going to do and that you will answer questions at the end.

Activity: All right on the night?

Read the following account and answer the questions that follow. If possible, compare ideas with a friend in your class.

Gemma looked around in exasperation. The team were on the final rehearsal of their presentation and nothing was going right. Amaya seemed to think it was funny. 'Honestly, Gemma, why don't you just chill for a bit?' she suggested. 'You know what they say – a bad dress rehearsal means we'll do really well tomorrow!'

Gemma glared at her. 'Well, can I make a suggestion, too, Amaya,' she retorted. 'Why don't you just concentrate for a change? Sprawling around and dissolving into giggles every five minutes isn't helping either.'

She turned to Adam. 'And I thought you were going to build a simple model,' she said, 'not one that falls apart every time you touch it.'

Adam looked crest-fallen. 'But I wanted to show how it worked.'

'How it's supposed to work, you mean!' raged Gemma, all her worries and anxieties now coming to the fore. 'We'll look stupid if it ends up in bits on the floor tomorrow and Amaya just falls about laughing again.'

'And Imran,' continued Gemma, turning her sights on the last member of the team, 'why is it so difficult for you to count to three minutes? We've agreed over and over again we'll each talk for three minutes and every time you get carried away with the sound of your own voice and talk for twice as long. It just means we're going to overrun and get penalised. And stop trying to wriggle out of answering questions properly. For heaven's sake, if you don't know the answer, how hard is it just to say so?'

Silence fell. No-one looked at each other. Adam fiddled with his model and something else fell off. Amaya wanted to laugh but didn't dare.

Imran was sulking and vowed never to say anything ever again. 'You wait,' he thought. 'Tomorrow I'll race through my part in one minute flat. And then what are you going to do?'

1 Identify the strengths and weaknesses of each member of the presentation team.

Name	Strengths	Weaknesses
Gemma		
Amaya		
Adam		
Imran		

2 What have the team done right, so far, in getting ready for their presentation?

3 Why do you think they are having problems?

4 If you were Gemma's tutor, what advice would you give her at this point?

Activity: Group presentation

Your team recently conducted an investigation into the verbal and non-verbal methods of communication used in business. You have now been asked to make a group presentation on your findings. There are five members in your team and the following tasks have to be completed:

1 pull together research on verbal and non-verbal communication

2 allocate individual responsibilities

3 obtain equipment and resources

4 decide timings and who will present what

5 visit and check presentation location

6 prepare PowerPoint slides and handouts

7 rehearse.

If you were the team leader, how would you approach each of the seven tasks?

1

2

3

4

Step Ten: Maximise your opportunities and manage your problems

Case study: Maximising opportunities

Ahmed has recently finished his BTEC National in Business. His tutor has asked whether he would be willing to give a short talk to the learners who have just started the programme. The talk will be about how to maximise the opportunities that arise on the course, and how to manage problems.

Ahmed starts by listing events that were good opportunities. He remembers that, when the class was taken on visits to various businesses, he was able to note lots of useful information.

When visiting speakers came to give talks to the class, he thought about questions to ask in advance and, again, took lots of notes. Ahmed's work experience also provided opportunities to gather information, as did his part-time job at a local supermarket. Finally, there are many television programmes, newspapers and journals that he found very useful when he was on the course.

As far as problems were concerned, thankfully he did not have too many. His worst occurred

at the beginning of his second year, when he broke his hand playing rugby. The tutors were very supportive and gave him extra time to complete assignments. Some of his friends on the course were not so fortunate and did experience more serious problems. They were helped considerably by professional counsellors and, of course, by the tutors. He remembers that many of the problems other learners faced were solved with reference to the existing college procedures which were explained clearly during the course induction.

Reflection points

Do you have the confidence to make best use of the opportunities presented to you?

Think about a problem you have had in the past and assess how you dealt with it. Could you improve your approach to tackling problems?

If your course takes one or two years to complete, then it is highly likely that you will experience some highs and lows in that time. You may find one or two topics harder than the rest. There may be distractions in your personal life to cope with. All of which means than you may not always be able to do your best.

It is, therefore, sensible to have an action plan to help you cope. It's also wise to plan how to make the best of opportunities for additional

experiences or learning. This section shows you how to do this.

TOP TIP

Because life rarely runs smoothly, it's sensible to capitalise on the opportunities that come your way and have a plan to deal with problems.

Making the most of your opportunities

There will be many opportunities for learning on your course, not all of which will be in school or college. You should prepare for some of the following to maximise the opportunities that each offer.

- **External visits**. Prepare in advance by reading about relevant topics. Make notes when you are there. Write up your notes neatly and file them safely for future reference.

- **Visiting speakers**. Questions can usually be submitted to the speaker in advance. Think carefully about information that you would find helpful. Make notes, unless someone has been appointed to make notes for the whole group. You may be asked to thank the speaker on behalf of your group.

- **Work experience**. If work experience is an essential part of your course, your tutor will help you to organise your placement and tell you about the evidence you need to obtain. You may also get a special logbook in which to record your experiences. Read and re-read the units to which your evidence will apply and make sure you understand the grading criteria and what you need to obtain. Make time to write up your notes, logbook and/or diary every night (if possible), while everything is fresh in your mind.

- **In your own workplace**. If you have a full-time or part-time job, watch for opportunities to find out more about relevant topics that relate to your course, such as health and safety, teamwork, dealing with customers, IT security and communications. Your employer will have had to address all of these issues. Finding out more about these issues will broaden your knowledge and give more depth to your assessment responses.

- **Television, newspapers, podcasts and other information sources**. The media can be an invaluable source of information. Look out for news bulletins relating to your studies, as well as information in topical television programmes – from *The Apprentice* to *Top Gear*. You can also read news headlines online (see page 69). Podcasts are useful, too. It will help if you know what topics you will be studying in the months to come, so you can spot useful opportunities as they arise.

TOP TIP

Remember that you can use online catch-up services, such as the BBC iPlayer or 4oD (for Channel 4 shows) to see TV programmes you have missed recently.

Minimising problems

Hopefully, any problems you experience during your course will only be minor; such as struggling to find an acceptable working method with someone in your team.

You should already know who to talk to about these issues, and who to go to if that person is absent or you would prefer to talk to someone else. If your problems are affecting your work, it's sensible to see your tutor promptly. It is a rare learner who is enthusiastic about every topic and gets on well with everyone else doing the course, so your tutor won't be surprised and will give you useful guidance (in confidence) to help.

TOP TIP

Don't delay talking to someone in confidence if you have a serious problem. If your course tutor is unavailable, talk to another staff member you like and trust.

Other sources of help

If you are unfortunate enough to have a more serious personal problem, the following sources of help may be available in your centre.

- **Professional counselling.** There may be a professional counselling service. If you see a counsellor, nothing you say during the session can be mentioned to another member of staff without your permission.

- **Complaint procedures.** If you have a serious complaint, the first step is to talk to your tutor. If you can't resolve your problem informally, there will be a formal learner complaint procedure. These procedures are used only for serious issues, not for minor difficulties.

- **Appeals procedures.** If you disagree with your final grade for an assignment, check the grading criteria and ask the subject tutor to explain how the grade was awarded. If you are still unhappy, talk to your personal tutor. If you still disagree, you have the right to make a formal appeal.

- **Disciplinary procedures.** These exist for when learners consistently flout a centre's rules and ensure that all learners are dealt with in the same way. Hopefully, you will never get into trouble, but you should make sure that you read these procedures carefully to see what could happen if you did. Remember that being honest and making a swift apology is always the wisest course of action.

- **Serious illness.** Whether this involves you, a family member or a close friend, it could affect your attendance. Discuss the problem with your tutor promptly; you will be missing information from the first day you are absent. There are many solutions in this type of situation – such as sending notes by post and updating you electronically (providing you are well enough to cope with the work).

TOP TIP

It's important to know your centre's procedures for dealing with important issues such as complaints, major illnesses, learner appeals and disciplinary matters.

Key points

- Don't miss opportunities to learn more about relevant topics through external visits, listening to visiting speakers, work experience, being at work or even watching television.

- If you have difficulties or concerns, talk to your tutor, or another appropriate person, promptly to make sure your work isn't affected.

Action points

1 Prepare in advance to maximise your opportunities.
   a) List the opportunities available on your course for obtaining more information and talking to experts. You can check with your tutor to make sure you've identified them all.

   b) Check the content of each unit you will be studying so that you know the main topics and focus of each.

   c) Identify the information that may be relevant to your course on television, on radio, in newspapers and in podcasts.

2 Make sure you know how to cope if you have a serious problem.
   a) Check your centre's procedures so you know who to talk to in a crisis, and who to contact if that person is absent.

   b) Find out where you can get hold of a copy of the main procedures in your centre that might affect you if you have a serious problem. Then read them.

Activity: Opportunities and problems

Here is a list of possible opportunities and potential problems that could occur while you are studying on the BTEC National in Business. Write notes on each of these five situations to explain how you would maximise the opportunity provided or manage the problem. Give clear reasons to justify your approach in each case.

1 A talk is being given at a nearby university on the state of the local business economy.

2 There are a number of work experience opportunities available at a local financial services company.

3 Your mother is going into hospital for two weeks and you may have to stay at home to look after your younger brother and sister.

4 The school is organising a visit to a distribution depot of a major supermarket.

5 The football team you play for is going on a week-long tour of Ireland during term time.

TOP TIP

The time and effort you will be putting into this course deserves to be rewarded. Make sure you know how to confront and successfully overcome problems.

AND FINALLY ...

Refer to this Study Skills Guide whenever you need to remind yourself about something related to your course. Keep it in a safe place so that you can use it whenever you need to refresh your memory. That way, you'll get the very best out of your course – and yourself!

Your Study Skills Guide will support you while you develop the skills you need for success in business, like interview skills.

Skills building

This section has been written to help you improve the skills needed to do your best in your assignments. You may be excellent at some skills already, others may need further work. The skills you can expect to demonstrate on your course include:

- your personal, learning and thinking skills (**PLTS**)
- your **functional skills** of ICT, maths/numeracy and English
- your proofreading and document production skills.

Personal, learning and thinking skills (PLTS)

These are the skills, personal qualities and behaviour that enable you to operate more independently, work more confidently with other people and be more effective at work. You'll develop these on your BTEC Level 3 National course through a variety of experiences and as you take on different roles and responsibilities.

The skills are divided into six groups:

1 **Independent enquirers** can process and evaluate information they investigate from different perspectives. They can plan what to do and how to do it, and take into account the consequences of making different decisions.

2 **Creative thinkers** generate and explore different ideas. They make connections between ideas, events and experiences that enable them to be inventive and imaginative.

3 **Reflective learners** can assess themselves and other people. They can evaluate their own strengths and limitations. They set themselves realistic goals, monitor their own performance and welcome feedback.

4 **Team workers** collaborate with other people to achieve common goals. They are fair and considerate to others, whether as a team leader or team member, and take account of different opinions.

5 **Self-managers** are well-organised and show personal responsibility, initiative, creativity and enterprise. They look for new challenges and responsibilities and are flexible when priorities change.

6 **Effective participators** play a full part in the life of their school, college, workplace or wider community by taking responsible action to bring improvements for others as well as themselves.

Action points

1 Many parts of this Study Skills Guide relate to the development of your own personal, learning and thinking skills. For each of the following, suggest the main skill groups to which the chapter relates. Refer to the box above and write a number next to each chapter title below.

a) Use your time wisely. ____

b) Understand how to research and analyse information. ____

c) Work productively as a member of a group. ____

d) Understand yourself. ____

e) Utilise all your resources. ____

f) Maximise your opportunities and manage your problems. ____

2 You have been on your BTEC National course for a few months now and, although everyone is enjoying the work, you realise that some of the learners have complaints.

Firstly, several learners object to an increase in the price of printouts and photocopying, on the basis that they can't do good work for their assignments if this is too expensive. You disagree and think that the prices are reasonable, given the cost of paper.

Secondly, a timetable change means your 2 pm – 4 pm Friday afternoon class has been moved to 9 am – 11 am. Some learners are annoyed and want it changed back, while others are delighted.

a) For the first problem, identify four factors which could indicate that those complaining about the price rise might be justified.

1

2

3

4

b) For the second problem:

  i) Think about which learners in your group would be most affected by the timetable change. Who might be most disturbed? Who might benefit from the earlier start?

  ii) Try to think of a creative solution, or compromise, that would please both groups.

c) During the discussions about these issues, some quieter members of the class are often shouted down by the more excitable members. Suggest a strategy for dealing with this, which everyone is likely to accept.

You can also check your ideas with the suggestions given on page 91.

3 a) Complete the chart opposite, identifying occasions when you may need to demonstrate personal, learning and thinking skills in your future career. Alternatively, apply each area to a part-time job you are currently doing.

b) Identify areas where you think you are quite strong and put a tick in the 'S' column. Check that you could provide evidence to support this judgement, such as a time when you have demonstrated this skill.

c) Now consider areas where you are not so good and put a cross in the 'W' column.

d) Then practise self-management by identifying two appropriate goals to achieve over the next month and make a note of them in the space provided. If possible, talk through your ideas at your next individual tutorial.

Personal, learning and thinking skills for future career/current part-time job				
Skill group	**Example skills**	**Occasions when you use/ will use skill**	**S**	**W**
Independent enquirers	Finding information Solving problems Making decisions Reconciling conflicting information or views Justifying decisions			
Creative thinkers	Finding imaginative solutions Making original connections Finding new ways to do something Opportunities for being innovative and inventive			
Reflective learners	Goals you may set yourself Reviewing your own progress Encouraging feedback Dealing with setbacks or criticism			
Team workers	Working with others Coping with different views to your own Adapting your behaviour Being fair and considerate			
Self-managers	Being self-starting and showing initiative Dealing positively with changing priorities Organising your own time and resources Dealing with pressure Managing your emotions			
Effective participators	Identifying issues of concern to others Proposing ways forward Identifying improvements for others Influencing other people Putting forward a persuasive argument			
Goals	1			
	2			

Functional skills

Functional skills are practical skills that everyone needs to have in order to study and work effectively. They involve using and applying English, maths and ICT.

Improving your literacy skills

Your written English communication skills

A good vocabulary increases your ability to explain yourself clearly. Work that is presented without spelling and punctuation errors looks professional, and increases the likelihood of someone understanding your intended meaning. Your written communication skills will be tested in many assignments. You should work at improving areas of weakness, such as spelling, punctuation or vocabulary.

Try the following to help you improve your written communication skills:

- Read more as this introduces you to new words, and it will help your spelling.
- Look up new words in a dictionary and try to use them in conversation.
- Use a Thesaurus (you can access one electronically in Word) to find alternatives to words you use a lot, this adds variety to your work.
- Never use words you don't understand in the hope that they sound impressive.
- Write neatly, so people can read what you've written.
- Do crosswords to improve your word power and spelling.
- Improve your punctuation – especially the use of apostrophes – either by using an online programme or by using a communication textbook.
- See page 92 for how to gain access to some helpful websites.

Verbal and non-verbal communication (NVC) skills

Talking appropriately means using the right words and 'tone'; using the right body language means sending positive signals to reinforce this message – such as smiling at someone when you say 'Hello'. Both verbal and non-verbal communication skills are essential when dealing with people at work.

The following are some hints for successful communication:

- Be polite, tactful and sensitive to other people's feelings.
- Think about the words and phrases that you like to hear, and use them when communicating with other people.
- Use simple language so that people can understand you easily. Explain what you mean, when necessary.
- Speak at the right pace. Don't speak so slowly that everyone loses interest, or so fast that no-one can understand you.
- Speak loudly enough for people to hear you clearly – but don't shout!
- Think about the specific needs of different people – whether you are talking to a senior manager, an important client, a shy colleague or an angry customer.
- Recognise the importance of non-verbal communication (NVC) so that you send positive signals by smiling, making eye contact, giving an encouraging nod or leaning forwards to show interest.
- Read other people's body language to spot if they are anxious or impatient so that you can react appropriately.

TOP TIP

Make sure you use the right tone for the person you're talking to. Would you talk to an adult in the same way you'd talk to a very young child?

Action points

1 See page 92 for how to gain access to websites which can help you to improve your literacy skills.

2 A battery made in China contained the following information.

> **DO NOT CONNECT IMPROPERLY**
>
> **CHARGE OR DISPOSE OF IN FIRE**

a) Can you see any problems with this? Give a reason for your answer.

b) Reword the information so that it is unambiguous.

3 If you ever thought you could completely trust the spellchecker on your computer, type the text given in box A on the next page into your computer. Your spellchecker will not highlight a single error; yet even at a glance you should be able to spot dozens of errors!

Read the passage in box A and try to understand it. Then rewrite it in box B on the next page without spelling, grammatical or punctuation errors. Compare your finished work with the suggested version on page 91.

Box A

> Anyone desirable to write books or reports, be they short or long, should strive too maximise they're optimal use of one's English grammar and obliviously there is an need for correct spelling two one should not neglect punctuation neither.
>
> Frequent lea, many people and individuals become confusing or just do not no it, when righting, when words that mean different, when sounding identically, or when pronounced very similar, are knot too bee spelled inn the same whey. The quay two suck seeding is dew care, a lack off witch Leeds too Miss Spellings that mite otherwise of bean a voided. Spell chequers donut find awl missed takes.
>
> Despite all the pitfalls how ever, with practise, patients and the right altitude, any one can soon become a grate writer and speaker, as what I did.

Box B Now rewrite the passage in the space below without errors.

4 In each of the statements listed in the table below, suggest what the body language described might mean.

Statement	What might this body language mean?
a) You are talking to your manager when he steps away from you and crosses his arms over his chest.	
b) You are talking to your friend about what she did at the weekend but she's avoiding making eye contact with you.	
c) During a tutorial session, your tutor is constantly tapping his fingers on the arm of his chair.	
d) Whenever you talk to your friend about your next assignment she bites her lower lip.	

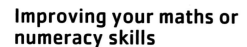

Improving your maths or numeracy skills

If you think numeracy isn't relevant to you, then think again! Numeracy is an essential life skill. If you can't carry out basic calculations accurately then you will have problems, perhaps when you least expect them. You'll often encounter numbers in various contexts – sometimes they will be correctly given, sometimes not. Unless you have a basic understanding about numeracy, you won't be able to tell the difference.

Good numeracy skills will improve your ability to express yourself, especially in assignments and at work. If you have problems, there are strategies that you can practise to help:

- Do basic calculations in your head, then check them on a calculator.

- Ask your tutor for help if important calculations give you problems.

- When you are using your computer, use the onscreen calculator (or a spreadsheet package) to do calculations.

- Investigate puzzle sites and brain training software, such as Dr Kageyama's Maths Training by Nintendo.

Action points

1 See page 92 for how to gain access to websites which can help you to improve your numeracy skills.

2 Try the following task with a friend or family member.

Each of you should write down 36 simple calculations in a list, e.g. 8 × 6, 19 – 8, 14 + 6. Exchange lists. See who can answer the most calculations correctly in the shortest time.

3 Figures aren't always what they appear to be. For example, Sophie watches *Who Wants To Be A Millionaire?* She hears Chris Tarrant say that there have been over 500 shows, with 1200 contestants who have each won over £50,000 on average. Five people have won £1 million.

Sophie says she is going to enter because she is almost certain to win more than £50,000 and could even win a million pounds.

a) On the figures given, what is the approximate total of money won over 500 shows (to the nearest £ million)?

b) Assuming that Sophie is chosen to appear on the show, and makes it on air as a contestant, do you think Sophie's argument that she will 'almost certainly' win more than £50,000 is correct? Give a reason for your answer. (The correct answer is on page 92.)

4 You have a part-time job and have been asked to carry out a survey on the usage of the drinks vending machine. You decide to survey 500 people, and find that:

- 225 use the machine to buy one cup of coffee per day only

- 100 use the machine to buy one cup of tea per day only

- 75 use the machine to buy one cup of cold drink per day only

- 50 use the machine to buy one cup of hot chocolate per day only

- the rest are non-users

- the ratio of male to female users is 2:1.

a) How many men in your survey use the machine?

b) How many women in your survey use the machine?

c) Calculate the proportion of the people in your survey that use the machine. Express this as a fraction and as a percentage.

d) What is the ratio of coffee drinkers to tea drinkers in your survey?

e) What is the ratio of coffee drinkers to hot chocolate drinkers in your survey?

f) If people continue to purchase from the machine in the same ratio found in your survey, and last month 1800 cups of coffee were sold, what would you expect the sales of the cold drinks to be?

g) Using the answer to f), if coffee costs 65p and all cold drinks cost 60p, how much would have been spent in total last month on these two items?

Improving your ICT skills

Good ICT skills are an asset in many aspects of your daily life and not just for those studying to be IT practitioners.

The following are ways in which you can Improve your ICT skills:

- Check that you can use the main features of the software packages you need to produce your assignments, eg Word, Excel and PowerPoint.
- Choose a good search engine and learn to use it properly. Go to page 92 for information on how to access a useful website.
- Developing and using your IT skills enables you to enhance your assignments. This may include learning how to import and export text and artwork from one package to another; taking digital photographs and inserting them into your work and/or creating drawings or diagrams by using appropriate software.

Action points

1 Check your basic knowledge of IT terminology by identifying each of these items on your computer screen:

a) taskbar	**f)** scroll bars
b) toolbar	**g)** status bar
c) title bar	**h)** insertion point
d) menu bar	**i)** maximise/
e) mouse pointer	minimise button.

2 Assess your IT skills by identifying the packages and operations you find easy to use and those that you find more difficult. If you use Microsoft Office products (Word, PowerPoint, Access or Excel) you can find out more about improving your skills online. Go to page 92 for information on how to access a useful website.

3 Search the internet to find a useful dictionary of IT terms. Bookmark it for future use. Find out the meaning of any of the following terms that you don't know already:

a) portal

b) cached link

c) home page

d) browser

e) firewall

f) HTML

g) URL

h) cookie

i) hyperlink

j) freeware.

Proofreading and document preparation skills

Improving your keyboard, document production and general IT skills can save you hours of time. When you have good skills, the work you produce will be of a far more professional standard.

- Think about learning to touch type. Your centre may have a workshop you can join, or you can use an online program – go to page 92 for information on how to access a useful website. From here you can access websites that will allow you to test and work on improving your typing skills.

- Obtain correct examples of any document formats you will have to use, such as a report or summary, either from your tutor, the internet or from a textbook.

- Proofread all your work carefully. A spellchecker won't find all your mistakes, so you must read through it yourself as well.

- Make sure your work looks professional by using a suitable typeface and font size, as well as reasonable margins.

- Print your work and store the printouts neatly, so that it stays in perfect condition for when you hand it in.

Action points

1 You can check and improve your typing skills using online typing sites – see link in previous section.

2 Check your ability to create documents by scoring yourself out of 5 for each of the following questions, where 5 is something you can do easily and 0 is something you can't do at all. Then focus on improving every score where you rated yourself 3 or less.

I know how to:

a) create a new document and open a saved document _____

b) use the mouse to click, double-click and drag objects _____

c) use drop-down menus _____

d) customise my toolbars by adding or deleting options _____

e) save and/or print a document _____

f) create folders and sub-folders to organise my work _____

g) move a folder I use regularly to My Places _____

h) amend text in a document _____

i) select, copy, paste and delete information in a document _____

j) quickly find and replace text in a document _____

k) insert special characters _____

l) create a table or insert a diagram in a document _____

m) change the text size, font and colour _____

n) add bold, italics or underscore _____

o) create a bullet or numbered list _____

p) align text left, right or centred _____

q) format pages before they are printed _____

r) proofread a document so that there are no mistakes _____.

Answers

Activity: Let's give you a tip... (page 68)

a) i) Fact

ii) Opinion – the number cannot be validated

iii) Fact

iv) Opinion

v) Opinion

vi) Opinion – again the number is estimated

Skills building answers

PLTS action points (page 81)

1 a) Use your time wisely = **5** Self-managers

b) Understand how to research and analyse information = **1** Independent enquirers, **5** Self-managers

c) Work productively as a member of a group = **4** Team workers, **6** Effective participators

d) Understand yourself = **3** Reflective learners

e) Utilise all your resources = **5** Self-managers

f) Maximise your opportunities and manage your problems = **1** Independent enquirers, **2** Creative thinkers, **3** Reflective learners, **5** Self-managers

2 a) Factors to consider in relation to the increased photocopying/printing charges include: the comparative prices charged by other schools/colleges, how often there is a price rise, whether any printing or photocopying at all can be done without charge, whether there are any concessions for special tasks or assignments, the availability of class sets of books/popular library books for loan (which reduces the need for photocopying.)

b) i) An earlier start will be more likely to negatively affect those who live further away and who are reliant on public transport, particularly in rural areas. The earlier finish will benefit anyone who has a part-time job that starts on a Friday afternoon or who has after college commitments, such as looking after younger sisters or brothers.

ii) The scope for compromise would depend on whether there are any classes between 11 am and 2 pm on a Friday, whether tutors had any flexibility and whether the new 9 am – 11 am class could be moved to another time or day.

c) One strategy would be to allow discussion for a set time, ensure everyone had spoken, then put the issue to a vote. The leader should prompt suggestions from quieter members by asking people individually what they think.

Literacy skills action points (page 85)

2 a) The statement reads as if it is acceptable to either charge it or dispose of it in fire.

b) Do not connect this battery improperly. Do not recharge it and do not dispose of it in fire.

3 Anyone who wishes to write books or reports, whether short or long, should try to use English grammatically. Obviously there is a need for correct spelling, too. Punctuation should also not be neglected.

Frequently, people confuse words with different meanings when they are writing, especially when these sound identical or very similar, even when they must not be spelled in the same way. The key to succeeding is due care, a lack of which leads to misspellings that might otherwise have been avoided. Spellcheckers do not find all mistakes.

Despite all the pitfalls, however, with practice, patience and the right attitude, anyone can soon become a great writer and speaker, like me.

4 (Possible answers)

a) Stepping backwards and crossing arms across the chest might indicate that your manager is creating a barrier between you and himself or that he is angry.

b) Your friend might be feeling guilty about what she did at the weekend or not confident that you will approve of what she tells you.

c) Your tutor might be frustrated as he has many things to do and so wants the tutorial to be over quickly.

d) Your friend might be anxious about the next assignment or about the time she has to complete it.

Numeracy action points (page 88)

3 a) £60 million

b) Sophie's argument is incorrect as £50,000 is an average, i.e. some contestants will win more, but many will win less. The distribution of prize money is greater at lower amounts because more people win small amounts of money than large amounts – and only five have won the top prize of £1 million.

4 a) 300

b) 150

c) 9/10ths, 90%

d) 225:100 (= 45:20) = 9:4

e) 225:50 = 9:2

f) 600

g) £1530

Accessing website links

Links to various websites are referred to throughout this BTEC Level 3 National Study Skills Guide. To ensure that these links are up-to-date, that they work and that the sites aren't inadvertently linked to any material that could be considered offensive, we have made the links available on our website: www.pearsonhotlinks.co.uk. When you visit the site, search either by the title BTEC Level 3 National Study Skills Guide in Business or ISBN 9781846905629. From here you can gain access to the website links and information on how they can be used to help you with your studies.

Useful terms

Accreditation of Prior Learning (APL)
Some of your previous achievements and experiences may be able to be used to count towards your qualification.

Apprenticeships
Schemes that enable you to work and earn money at the same time as you gain further qualifications (an NVQ award and a technical certificate) and improve your functional skills. Apprentices learn work-based skills relevant to their job role and their chosen industry. See page 92 for information on how to access a website where you can find out more.

Assessment methods
Techniques used to check that your work demonstrates the learning and understanding required for your qualification, such as assignments, case studies and practical tasks.

Assessor
An assessor is the tutor who marks or assesses your work.

Assignment
A complex task or mini-project set to meet specific grading criteria and learning outcomes.

Awarding body
An organisation responsible for devising, assessing and issuing qualifications. The awarding body for all BTEC qualifications is Edexcel.

Credit value
The number of credits attached to your BTEC course. The credit value increases in relation to the length of time you need to complete the course, from 30 credits for a BTEC Level 3 Certificate, 60 credits for a Subsidiary Diploma, 120 credits for a Diploma, up to 180 credits for an Extended Diploma.

Degrees
Higher education qualifications offered by universities and colleges. Foundation degrees take two years to complete; honours degrees may take three years or longer.

Department for Business Innovation and Skills (BIS)
BIS is responsible for further and higher education and skills training, as well as functions related to trade and industry. See page 92 for information on accessing a website to find out more.

Department for Education
The Department for Education is the government department responsible for schools and education, as well as for children's services.

Distance learning
When you learn and/or study for a qualification at home or at work. You communicate with your tutor and/or the centre that organises the course by post, telephone or electronically.

Educational Maintenance Award (EMA)
An EMA is a means-tested award that provides eligible learners under 19, who are studying a full-time course at school or college, with a cash sum of money every week. See page 92 for information on how to access a website where you can find out more.

External verification
Formal checking of the programme by an Edexcel representative that focuses on sampling various assignments to check content, accurate assessment and grading.

Forbidden combinations
There are some qualifications that cannot be taken simultaneously because their content is too similar.

Functional skills
Practical skills in English, maths and ICT that enable people to work confidently, effectively and independently. Level 2 Functional Skills are mapped to the units of BTEC Level 3 National qualifications. They aren't compulsory to achieve on the course, but are of great use.

Grade boundaries
Pre-set points that determine whether you will achieve a pass, merit or distinction as the overall final grade(s) for your qualification.

Grading criteria
The specific evidence you have to demonstrate to obtain a particular grade in the unit.

Grading domains
The main areas of learning that support the learning outcomes. On a BTEC Level 3 National course these are: application of knowledge and understanding; development of practical and technical skills; personal development for occupational roles; application of PLTS and functional skills.

Grading grid
The table in each unit of your qualification specification that sets out what you have to show you can do.

Higher education (HE)
Post-secondary and post-further education, usually provided by universities and colleges.

Higher-level skills
These are skills such as evaluating or critically assessing information. They are more difficult than lower-level skills such as writing a description or making a list. You must be able to demonstrate higher-level skills to achieve a distinction.

Indicative reading
Recommended books and journals whose content is both suitable and relevant for the BTEC unit studied.

Induction
A short programme of events at the start of a course designed to give you essential information, and introduce you to your fellow learners and tutors, so that you can settle down as quickly and easily as possible.

Internal verification
The quality checks carried out by nominated tutors at your school or college to ensure that all assignments are at the right level, cover appropriate learning outcomes and grading criteria, and that all assessors are marking work consistently and to the same standard.

Investors in People (IiP)
A national quality standard that sets a level of good practice for training and developing of people within a business. Participating organisations must demonstrate commitment to achieve the standard.

Learning outcomes
The knowledge and skills you must demonstrate to show that you have effectively learned a unit.

Learning support
Additional help that is available to all learners in a school or college who have learning difficulties or other special needs.

Levels of study
The depth, breadth and complexity of knowledge, understanding and skills required to achieve a qualification, which also determines its level. Level 2 equates to GCSE level and Level 3 equates to A-level. As you successfully achieve one level, you can then progress to the next. BTEC qualifications are offered at Entry Level, then Levels 1, 2, 3, 4 and 5.

Local Education Authority (LEA)
The local government body responsible for providing education for all learners of compulsory school age. The LEA is also responsible for managing the education budget for 16–19 learners in its area.

Mandatory units
These are units that all learners must complete to gain a qualification; in this case a BTEC Level 3 National. Some BTEC qualifications have an over-arching title, eg Construction, but within Construction you can choose different pathways. Your chosen pathway may have additional mandatory units specific to that pathway.

Mentor
A more experienced person who will guide you and counsel you if you have a problem or difficulty.

Mode of delivery
The way in which a qualification is offered to learners for example, part-time, full-time, as a short course or by distance learning.

National Occupational Standard (NOS)
Statements of the skills, knowledge and understanding you need to develop in order to be competent at a particular job.

National Vocational Qualification (NVQ)
Qualifications that concentrate on the practical skills and knowledge required to do a job competently. They are usually assessed in the workplace and range from Level 1 (the lowest) to Level 5 (the highest).

Nested qualifications

Qualifications that have 'common' units, so that learners can easily progress from one to another by adding on more units.

Ofqual

The public body responsible for regulating qualifications, exams and tests in England.

Optional units

Units on your course from which you may be able to make a choice. They help you specialise your skills, knowledge and understanding and may help progression into work or further education.

Pathway

All BTEC Level 3 National qualifications comprise a small number of mandatory units and a larger number of optional units. These units are grouped into different combinations to provide alternative pathways to achieving the qualification. These pathways are usually linked to different career preferences.

Peer review

This involves feedback on your performance by your peers (members of your team, or class group.) You will also be given an opportunity to review their performance.

Plagiarism

The practice of copying someone else's work, or work from any other sources (eg the internet), and passing it off as your own. This practice is strictly forbidden on all courses.

Personal, learning and thinking skills (PLTS)

The skills, personal qualities and behaviour that improve your ability to work independently. Developing these skills makes you more effective and confident at work. Opportunities for developing these skills are a feature of all BTEC Level 3 National courses. These skills aren't compulsory to achieve on the course, but are of great use to you.

Portfolio

A collection of work compiled by a learner, usually as evidence of learning, to present to an assessor.

Procrastinator

Someone who is forever putting off or delaying work, either because they are lazy or because they have poor organisational skills.

Professional body

An organisation that exists to promote or support a particular profession; for example, the Royal Institute of British Architects (RIBA).

Professional development and training

This involves undertaking activities relevant to your job to increase and/or update your knowledge and skills.

Project

A project is a comprehensive piece of work, which normally involves original research and investigation by an individual or by a team. The findings and results may be presented in writing and summarised as a presentation.

Qualifications and Credit Framework (QCF)

The QCF is a framework for recognising skills and qualifications. It does this by awarding credit for qualifications and units so that they are easier to measure and compare. All BTEC Level 3 National qualifications are part of the QCF.

Qualifications and Curriculum Development Agency (QCDA)

The QCDA is responsible for maintaining and developing the national curriculum, delivering assessments, tests and examinations and reforming qualifications.

Quality assurance

In education, this is the process of continually checking that a course of study is meeting the specific requirements set down by the awarding body.

Sector Skills Councils (SSCs)

The 25 employer-led, independent organisations responsible for improving workforce skills in the UK by identifying skill gaps and improving learning in the workplace. Each council covers a different type of industry.

Semester

Many universities and colleges divide their academic year into two halves or semesters, one from September to January and one from February to July.

Seminar

A learning event involving a group of learners and a tutor, which may be learner-led, and follow research into a topic that has been introduced at an earlier stage.

Study buddy

A person in your group or class who takes notes for you and keeps you informed of important developments if you are absent. You do the same for them in return.

Time-constrained assignment

An assessment you must complete within a fixed time limit.

Tutorial

An individual or small group meeting with your tutor at which you can discuss your current work and other more general course issues. At an individual tutorial, your progress on the course will be discussed and you can raise any concerns or personal worries you may have.

The University and Colleges Admissions Service (UCAS)

UCAS (pronounced 'you-cass') is the central organisation that processes all applications for higher education (HE) courses.

UCAS points

The number of points allocated by UCAS for the qualifications you have obtained. Higher education institutions specify how many points you need to be accepted on the courses they offer. See page 92 for information on how to access a website where you can find out more.

Unit abstract

The summary at the start of each BTEC unit that tells you what the unit is about.

Unit content

Details about the topics covered by the unit and the knowledge and skills you need to complete it.

Unit points

The number of points you gain when you complete a unit. These will depend on the grade you achieve (pass, merit or distinction).

Vocational qualification

Designed to develop knowledge and understanding relevant to a chosen area of work.

Work experience

Time you spend on an employer's premises when you learn about the enterprise, carry out work-based tasks and develop skills and knowledge.

Please note that all information given within these useful terms was correct at the time of going to print.